RAND NATIONAL DEFENSE RESEARC

# Exploring the Role Nuclear Weapons Could Play in Deterring Russian Threats to the Baltic States

Paul K. Davis, J. Michael Gilmore, David R. Frelinger, Edward Geist, Christopher K. Gilmore, Jenny Oberholtzer, Danielle C. Tarraf

For more information on this publication, visit www.rand.org/t/RR2781

**Library of Congress Cataloging-in-Publication Data** is available for this publication.
ISBN: 978-1-9774-0215-8

Published by the RAND Corporation, Santa Monica, Calif.


*Cover: pavlofox/stock.adobe.com.*

# Preface

This report assesses nonstrategic nuclear options for bolstering deterrence capabilities in the Baltic states (Estonia, Latvia, and Lithuania). Interest in such options has been stimulated by concerns about potential Russian aggression against these nations, which are members of the North Atlantic Treaty Organization, and by Russia's vigorous efforts to modernize and diversify its nuclear capabilities for limited war. The most recent U.S. Nuclear Posture Review described several U.S. nuclear initiatives that are either underway or proposed. The report should be of interest to senior decisionmakers across the U.S. Department of Defense, as well as to members of Congress.

## RAND Ventures

The RAND Corporation is a research organization that develops solutions to public policy challenges to help make communities throughout the world safer and more secure, healthier and more prosperous. RAND is nonprofit, nonpartisan, and committed to the public interest.

RAND Ventures is a vehicle for investing in policy solutions. Philanthropic contributions support our ability to take the long view, tackle tough and often controversial topics, and share our findings in innovative and compelling ways. RAND's research findings and recommendations are based on data and evidence and therefore do not necessarily reflect the policy preferences or interests of its clients, donors, or supporters.

Funding for this venture was made possible by the independent research and development provisions of RAND's contracts for the operation of its U.S. Department of Defense federally funded research and development centers. The project was overseen by RAND's International Security and Defense Policy Center, which analyzes changes in the international political, strategic, economic, and technological environment and helps DoD develop policies to shape the environment and advance U.S. interests. For more information about RAND and ISDP, see www.rand.org (contact information is provided on the webpage).

# Contents

# Figures and Tables

## Figures

## Tables

# Summary

Previous analysis has shown that, given the North Atlantic Treaty Organization (NATO)'s current substantial disadvantage in conventional forces for a conflict in the Baltic states (Estonia, Latvia, and Lithuania), a Russian invasion there would reach some or all of the capitals within a few days, presenting NATO with a fait accompli. As outlined in the 2018 Nuclear Posture Review, the United States is currently considering tailored deterrence strategies, including options to use nuclear weapons to deter Russian aggression in the Baltic states. What role could the threatened use of nonstrategic nuclear weapons play in deterring such an invasion? What military and other outcomes would nuclear use accomplish, and what are the implications for credibly enhancing extended deterrence? In this report, we seek to answer these questions.

To do so, we first review deterrence theory and lessons from the Cold War to identify principles for thinking about the matter. We then draw contrasts with today's situation in the Baltic states. With that background, we discuss considerations in defining NATO options for limited nuclear use in a Baltic conflict. We consider a range of methods that might be used to evaluate such options but focus on wargaming because the project's limited resources did not permit more-extensive analytic activities. We describe the framing and setup for the wargame exercise that we conducted, results from the exercise, and related discussions (e.g., what the results would have been if events had unfolded differently). The primary insight from the wargame exercise is that, once nuclear exchanges begin in such a conflict, NATO would—from a military perspective—have much stronger incentives to seek war termination than Russia would. That is, NATO would lack escalation dominance, and Russia would have it. Although Russia might terminate the conflict anyway despite its local military advantages, it would seem unwise for NATO to count on that outcome. That said, in the wargame exercise, we sought to clarify more deliberately, *as a function of scenario details*, how much various NATO nuclear options might contribute to deterrence despite Russia's escalation dominance.

In our review of deterrence theory, we found that the most-relevant elements relate to extended deterrence and the broader challenge of deterring small or impulsive aggressions. NATO addressed these matters in the 1960s and 1970s, going to great lengths to improve the credibility of deterrence by introducing limited nuclear options and tightening linkages to the strategic nuclear umbrella. Doing so required integrated efforts on declaratory, employment, and programming strategies; on military doctrine; and on force postures and force practices in training and exercises. Although NATO still declares nuclear weapons to be an important element of its strategies and plans, it cannot realistically pursue such an integrated effort today. By contrast, Russia has cultivated its own deterrent strategy, which aims to combine a robust central deterrent with limited nuclear options for using nonstrategic and strategic nuclear forces in extreme circumstances. Under such circumstances, Russia might be able to credibly threaten the use of such options for dramatic military effect, not just to demonstrate resolve or salvage a bad situation. That is, Russia might escalate to *win* rather than just to bring about de-escalation.

Key differences between the current NATO versus Russia situation in the Baltic states and the Cold War confrontation between NATO and the Warsaw Pact include the following:

- A NATO and U.S. threat to escalate to general nuclear war over a Russian invasion of the Baltic states has doubtful credibility; in addition, the likelihood of such escalation occurring inevitably seems much smaller than in the Cold War settings.
- In a conflict in the Baltic states, Russian ground forces would greatly outnumber NATO ground forces. This fact and geogra-

phy are why Russia could invade one or more Baltic states and rapidly achieve its war aims using conventional forces alone, probably within a few days.

- Targets attacked by NATO using nonstrategic nuclear weapons would, from the outset of the war, be either in Russia proper or in NATO countries (i.e., the Baltic states). During the Cold War, NATO could (if it chose) conduct limited nuclear attacks against lucrative military targets in Warsaw Pact countries other than Russia throughout the conflict.
- NATO's military and military-supporting infrastructure was extensive, dispersed, and hardened to a greater extent during the Cold War than it is today.
- NATO combat with Russia in the Baltic states would require suppressing Russia's sophisticated air defense systems, but NATO would probably be unable to damage those defenses quickly enough to slow a rapid Russian advance to the Baltic capitals. Such attacks could trigger further escalation because Russia regards these systems as a strategic asset.

Development of a NATO and U.S. nuclear-based, tailored deterrence strategy necessitates finding the right balance among several key elements, including U.S. strategic nuclear and NATO's nonstrategic nuclear forces. Other balances must be struck regarding ground-based missiles, sea-based missiles, and dual-capable aircraft; the planning of limited nuclear use for stakes-raising, military effect, or both; and an emphasis on deterrence by stakes-raising or deterrence by nuclear war-fighting capability. Finding the right balance was not simple during the Cold War and is not simple today.

A credible deterrence strategy for NATO could include a combination of (1) improved conventional defense capabilities in the Baltic states; (2) improved capabilities for employing nuclear weapons in a Baltic conflict using existing or modified strategic platforms, as well as new dedicated platforms to deliver longer-range weapons and perhaps short-range weapons; (3) changes in planning, doctrine, and exercises to improve the feasibility, timeliness, and credibility of nuclear use; (4) improvements in NATO's military-related infrastructure, including dispersal and hardening of bases; and (5) options for horizontal escalation (i.e., escalation to other theaters in which Russia would be more disadvantaged). We were able to look at only some of these. Overall, our assessments are as follows:

- Despite NATO's large political, military, and economic advantages overall, which support general deterrence, the do-nothing option is risky because military deterrence in the Baltic states specifically is weak and generally questionable.
- Improvements to conventional forces have the highest priority; they could also enhance the value of some nuclear options. Some of these improvements are underway.
- Practiced options for extremely fast response without much strategic warning are important because Russia might otherwise find ways, using deception, to accomplish a short-warning fait accompli.
- Despite Russia's escalation dominance, the modernized nuclear options might be valuable in certain circumstances of crisis or conflict if Russian leaders have not already anticipated and discounted the significance of NATO's nuclear use (whether a first use or in response to Russian first use).
- Given the limited *military* value for modernized NATO nonstrategic nuclear weapons, some may question the priority of pursuing such modernization. However, modernized nuclear options would reduce Russian asymmetries in theater-nuclear matters—something that can be significant to public perceptions and the stability of domestic politics. Also, reducing nonstrategic nuclear weapon asymmetries might cause NATO allies to feel more assured of the credibility of U.S. security guarantees and might improve U.S. leverage in possible negotiations about nonstrategic nuclear weapons (the United States has very little leverage now). Finally, modernized nuclear options might be necessary for dealing with security challenges other than Russia.

Ultimately, judgments on such matters are for policymakers.

Overall, the military challenges for NATO are significant, as is the potential for high economic and political costs for the various strategies. Again, however, the do-nothing baseline is fraught with risk because Russia enjoys large military advantages and could aspire to a nearly painless aggression. NATO, aware of this, has been taking actions in the past few years. More action is necessary.

## Acknowledgments

We much appreciated reviews by Brad Roberts, director of the Lawrence Livermore National Laboratory's Center for Global Security Research, and by RAND colleague Stephen Flanagan, as well as numerous comments and suggestions in the course of the study by other RAND colleagues.

# Abbreviations

| | |
|---|---|
| ABCT | armored brigade combat team |
| ALCM | air-launched cruise missile |
| CBO | Congressional Budget Office |
| DoD | U.S. Department of Defense |
| FY | fiscal year |
| GAO | U.S. General Accounting Office |
| GLCM | ground-launched cruise missile |
| IADS | integrated air defense system |
| IBCT(ABN) | infantry brigade combat team (airborne) |
| NATO | North Atlantic Treaty Organization |
| NSNW | nonstrategic nuclear weapons |
| O&M | operations and maintenance |
| O&S | operations and support |
| OPTEMPO | operational tempo |
| RDT&E | research, development, test, and evaluation |
| R-FLEX | RAND Framework for Live Exercises |
| SBCT | Stryker brigade combat team |
| SLBM | submarine-launched ballistic missile |
| SLCM | submarine-launched cruise missile |
| SPMAGTF-CR | Special Purpose Marine Air Ground Task Force – Crisis Response |
| START | Strategic Arms Reduction Treaty |
| TLAM | Tomahawk Land-Attack Missile |

CHAPTER ONE

# Introduction

As demonstrated in past research (e.g., Shlapak and Johnson, 2016), a Russian invasion of the Baltic states would capture some or all capital cities within a few days, presenting the North Atlantic Treaty Organization (NATO) with a fait accompli. The United States is currently considering tailored deterrence strategies, including options to use nuclear weapons to deter Russian aggression in the Baltic states (U.S. Department of Defense [DoD], 2018). This raises the following important questions, which we address in this report:

- What role could the use of nonstrategic nuclear weapons (NSNW) play in deterring such an invasion?
- What military and other outcomes would nuclear use accomplish?
- What are the implications for credibly enhancing extended deterrence?

In this report, we review relevant deterrence theory, review military developments in or near the Baltic states and their implications for the outcome of a Russian invasion, use wargaming and qualitative modeling to describe the potential effects of Russia or NATO employing NSNW, and discuss implications for using NSNW to deter a Russian invasion.

In our review of deterrence theory, we draw lessons from the Cold War and more-fundamental theory. We then outline implications for the Russian threat to the Baltic states. The discussion concludes by summarizing qualitative and quantitative analytic methods, including wargaming, that can be useful in assessing deterrent options. We then discuss a wargaming exercise in which NSNW were employed during a Russian invasion of the Baltic states. The resulting insights highlight the reality that, even if NATO makes significant efforts to modernize its nonstrategic nuclear weapons, it would have much stronger military incentives to end a future war than Russia would. That is, Russia would still enjoy escalation dominance. Thus, modernizing NSNW alone will not compensate for the lack of NATO conventional ground forces capable of blunting a Russian invasion. Appendixes to this report provide rough cost estimates for selected new NSNW and for enhanced U.S. and NATO conventional ground forces.

This report is based on a small independent research project with limited resources. We believe that its conclusions about the military value of NSNW modernization being distinctly limited by major geographic and other asymmetries are solid. Other conclusions, however, are offered more tentatively because of subtleties that might be differently illuminated with more in-depth analysis. We suggest several such analyses that would be useful.

CHAPTER TWO

# Selective Review of Deterrence Theory

The literature on deterrence theory is voluminous, although the vast bulk of it was developed in the 20th century. Our report draws on a longer review (Davis et al., 2016) and a related National Research Council (2014) report, both of which note how different the current security environment is from that of the Cold War. Those sources also supplement standard literature by drawing on declassified government materials, books and journal articles by former policymakers, personal experiences of authors with in-government nuclear planning, and books relating specifically to the current era.

Our selection of material covers some fundamental issues, such as how deterrence can fail; differences of perspective that have divided nuclear strategists for nearly 70 years; and the special problems of *extended* deterrence, which have particular salience to the challenge that NATO faces in the Baltic states.

## Definitions

### Deterrence

The several definitions of *deterrence* are confusing. A common definition, with slight differences of wording across authors, is *the use of threats by one party to convince another party to refrain from initiating some course of action* (Morgan, 2003). When government leaders depend on this type of deterrence, they can run into several problems. First, the act of threatening is seen as provocative. Second, people often do not respond to threats in the way that those making the threats expect; pride, emotion, and anger come into play. Third, the threat of punishment cannot logically deter if the action threatened (e.g., to destroy al-Qaeda or the Islamic State) will be applied regardless of what the opponent does (Davis and Jenkins, 2002).

A broader and better definition of *deterrence* is a slight extension (adding the word *adequately*) of one proposed by Alexander L. George and Richard Smoke:

> Deterrence is the persuasion of one's opponent that the costs and/or risks of a given course of action he might take [*adequately*] outweigh its benefits. (George and Smoke, 1974, p. 11)

George and Smoke framed matters in terms of coercive diplomacy using a variety of means to *influence* the opponent's choices. Influences can be positive (offering inducements for some actions) or negative (threatening punishment or pointing out other likely negative consequences of other actions). Addressing influence is more powerful than threat-focused deterrence because it recognizes that all instruments of influence can be brought to bear, something recognized also in U.S. deterrence doctrine (U.S. Strategic Command, 2006). Thus, it may be preferable to use *deterrence* only when thinking about threats and *influence* only when thinking more generally; however, in this report, we use this broader meaning of deterrence (the modified definition from George and Smoke), which is consistent with official documents (Hagel, 2013, p. 4; DoD, 2018).

We have added *adequately* to George and Smoke's definition because there is no simple and objective calculation to be made. Adequacy is in the mind of the decisionmaker and may be assessed in a variety of ways: simple subtraction (benefits minus costs), a ratio criterion (e.g., benefits or costs exceed some threshold), a more complicated algorithm (e.g., costs exceed benefits and risks are less than a threshold), or some unstructured reasoning. How a given decisionmaker balances the various considerations will vary by individual and circumstance. Results may reflect limited rationality or even departures from rationality—for example, when an actor is driven strictly by an immediate emotion, such as desperation.

Figure 2.1 summarizes these concepts and the decisionmaking process when the adversary assesses courses of action. The figure uses the familiar convention of Side A attempting to influence Side B. Side A seeks to affect Side B's choice: Will B do something that A favors (left side) or will B take action that A seeks to avoid (right side)? The outcome will be determined by B's (perhaps) rational weighing of pros and cons derived from various factors. Side A's actions can influence some of those factors and thus affect Side B's assessment.

**Figure 2.1**
**An Adversary's Decisionmaking Process (Side A Attempts to Influence Side B)**

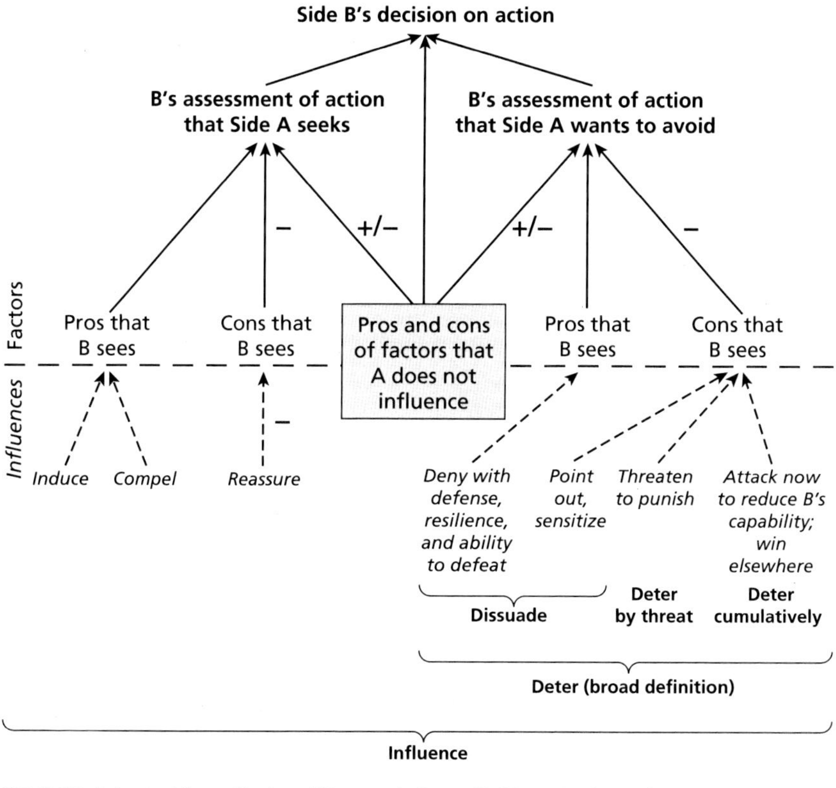


SOURCE: Adapted from National Research Council, 2014; Davis et al., 2016.
NOTES: As shown at the bottom of the figure, the broad definition of *deter* includes dissuade, deter by threat, and deter cumulatively. *Influence* includes all of those, as well as induce, compel, and reassure. The + and – signs on the arrows indicate the valence of influence.

The gray box in Figure 2.1 is a reminder that many factors influencing an opponent's actions are not readily subject to external influence. Internal politics, past history, and leaders' idiosyncrasies are examples of such factors. To Iranian revolutionaries seizing the U.S. embassy in 1979, the memory of the United States' role in overthrowing Iran's elected prime minister in 1953 loomed large (Byrne, 2014). Saddam Hussein's invasion of Kuwait in 1990 was driven more by contextual passions, anger, and Saddam's conspiratorial sense of threat than by a sober calculation of cost-effectiveness (Woods, 2008).

### Extended Deterrence

The most vexing problem of nuclear strategy during the Cold War was perhaps *extended deterrence*—that is, deterring an attack on an ally by an opponent. This strategy is inherently less credible than direct deterrence. As U.S. policymakers recognized early in the Cold War,

> Merely giving speeches and assurances to Western Europe would not necessarily be convincing [to allies]. Would the United States *really* initiate general nuclear war to protect Europe if it meant that the United States would suffer nuclear attack? The Europeans and NATO dealt with this profound issue in four ways: (1) Great Britain and France developed independent nuclear deterrent forces. (2) NATO developed and exercised a doctrine that intermingled conventional, theater-nuclear, and intercontinental nuclear forces—to include multi-national dual-capable nuclear weapons—which made escalation almost natural and therefore credible. (3) The United States led the effort to improve war-fighting capability of NATO conventional forces. (4) As part of the intermingling, NATO developed limited nuclear options that could be used to incentivize ending war, i.e., options to reestablish deterrence if conventional defense was failing. (Davis et al., 2016, p. 10; see also Legge, 2003; Delpech, 2012)

It is understandable that many people today do not recognize how much sustained effort was required years ago for NATO members to accomplish these things. Doing so meant enacting programs and activities that were potentially frightening to the countries' citizens and that were derided by many as unnecessary because deterrence was allegedly assured by the threat of assured destruction. Thus, NATO's efforts were raising a kind of devil's dilemma: Although NATO's increased willingness to use nuclear weapons might improve overall deterrence, it would raise the risk of nuclear war if war occurred at all.

## The Goal of Deterrence: Affecting Human Behavior

As Henry Kissinger observed, deterrence is about affecting human minds (Kissinger, 1966). (In the future, it might include affecting machine intelligence.) How does this occur? The early literature embraced the model of the rational actor assessing pros and cons, as in Figure 2.1. This model had intuitive appeal and allowed application of logic and game theory. Although the model continues to be useful, it can be misleading. It is better to consider separately how to affect decisions by (1) a rational actor, (2) an actor with only limited rationality, or (3) an irrational actor (Davis et al., 2016; National Research Council, 2014).

### Rational, Semirational, and Irrational Actors

The rational-actor model assumes that the actor assesses the pros and cons of diverse options and chooses the option with the greatest subjective expected utility. Using the model requires assuming a utility function and calculating its value for each option, based on assumptions about the world, option effectiveness, and so on. In the model, the option comparisons are subjective because, most importantly, utilities are subjective.

A model of limited (or semi-) rationality assumes that the actor attempts to behave like a rational actor but is beset by various problems. Assessments depend on perceptions of reality (e.g., motives of the opponent) that might be wrong, and options might be evaluated poorly because of the cognitive biases that affect humans (Kahneman, 2002; Jervis, Lebow, and Stein, 1985). Many systemic, societal, organizational, and bureaucratic factors have biasing influence, as do cognitive, affective, motivational, and characterological factors.[1] These factors can be partially reflected by adjusting inputs to a model structured like a rational-actor model. For example, someone at the Central Intelligence Agency might explain to a U.S. President that the target of a proposed deterrent action would likely interpret the action very differently from how it was intended.[2] Similarly, role-playing teams in wargames can highlight likely asymmetries of perception and values.

Irrational actors are less commonly discussed in the literature, despite historical failures of rationality resulting from real-world leaders suffering mental and physical problems, including debilitating illness (Yuri Andropov), alcohol abuse (Richard Nixon), paranoia (Joseph Stalin), and malignant narcissism (Saddam Hussein).[3] When behaviors reflect such problems, it makes no sense to rationalize the behaviors via utility functions; doing so amounts to vacuous, circular reasoning (e.g., "his behavior is understandable so long as we assume the right utility function, which we infer from observing his behavior").

### The Problem of Shifting Utilities

Another problem in using the rational-actor model is that it requires the assumption of stable utility functions or an understanding of how the utilities (i.e., values) are changing. Real people often do not even have stable utilities. In many cases, people discover their values in the course of experience, or, perhaps more accurately, values emerge as the result of experience, including human interactions. Even if no new values emerge, the emphasis on the various values changes with context, including history (e.g., when a decision is unduly affected by the most recent argument presented). Finally, everyone can do things that are driven by emotion and recognize later that those actions were

1 These factors can be represented with simple cognitive models (National Research Council, 2014), drawing on a body of earlier work (Davis and Arquilla, 1991; Davis, 1994).

2 Motivated bias (seeing what one wants to see in the information) sometimes looms large, such as with Saddam Hussein's reasoning in the lead-up to the Iraq War in 2003 and in the earlier 1990–1991 war (Woods et al., 2011). Such behavior can sometimes be predicted.

3 Referring to the deterrent of threatening assured destruction, Winston Churchill noted, "The deterrent does not cover the case of lunatics or dictators in the mood of Hitler when he found himself in his final dugout" (Churchill, 1955).

inconsistent with their best interest and longer-term values.[4] The phenomenon of changing utilities should be recognized when using the rational-actor, semirational-actor, and irrational-actor models.

Next, we outline some of the important elements of Cold War history bearing on deterrence.

## Selected Cold War History

In this section, we discuss parts of Cold War history relevant to our current study about deterring Russia from aggression against the Baltic states. Later, we examine the lessons learned from these events.

### Mutual Assured Destruction: Strategy or Curse

The profound national security implications of nuclear weapons were famously expressed by Bernard Brodie after World War II:

> Thus far the chief purpose of our military establishment has been to win wars. From now on its chief purpose must be to avert them. It can have almost no other useful purpose. (Brodie, 1946)

Deterring the Soviet Union in the 1950s was easy for the United States because it had a monopoly on nuclear weapons and a track record of using them. This reality was exploited by President Dwight D. Eisenhower as a way to avoid massive expenditures on conventional forces. However, that approach had only a short period of viability. By the late 1950s, the approach was persuasively criticized by Kissinger (1957) and others. Albert Wohlstetter, in his seminal paper on the delicate balance of terror, anticipated the rapid development of Soviet capabilities and made the following fundamental observations about deterrence (Wohlstetter, 1959):

---

4 See Davis et al., 2016; Payne, 2011; Morgan, 2003. See also National Research Council, 2014, Appendix E, which draws on literature about national leaders' decisionmaking; some of that literature is by Jerrold Post, who founded the CIA's leadership profiling unit and highlighted the concept of malignant narcissism.

- The key is survivable *second*-strike forces and, thus, assured retaliation.
- Achieving assured retaliation is very difficult, requiring careful designs and meticulous attention to detail.
- Deterrence by assured retaliation is vital but not enough.

What is often forgotten is that strategists never agreed about the desirability or acceptability of *mutual* assured destruction. Wohlstetter (1959) saw assured retaliation capability as essential, but he also supported civil defense, ballistic missile defense, and counterforce capability throughout his career (Wohlstetter, 1987). Even Brodie, often associated with more "dovish" positions, had nuanced views and great concerns about the problems of limited war and the necessity of being able to fight a war if it occurred. He observed,

> We also have to bear in mind that deterrence can fail. The fact that total war is definitely possible makes us revise our approach to limited war; instead of taking limitations for granted we have to recognize the possibly great difficulties in keeping war limited. These considerations underline the necessity for an independent limited war capability. The appreciable danger of total war also obliges us to consider the needs of civil defense. (Brodie, 1959)

Kissinger later elaborated on why relying on the threat of total destruction was unwise:

> The threat of all-out war purchases deterrence at an exorbitant risk. It requires us in every crisis to stake our survival on the credibility of a threat which we will be increasingly reluctant to implement and which, if implemented, will force us into the very kind of war our strategy should make every attempt to avoid. (Kissinger, 1957, p. 135)[5]

---

[5] Churchill's last speech to the UK House of Commons reflected similar concerns. On the one hand, he saw "defence through deterrents" as the only near-term strategy (Churchill, 1955, p. 3). At the same time, he recognized the need for effective conventional defenses to prevent limited encroachments (p. 7). And, because he saw war as possible, he supported civil defense (pp. 7–8).

Kissinger went on to argue,

> Strategy can assist policy only by developing a maximum number of stages between total peace (which may mean total surrender) and total war. It can increase the willingness of policy-makers to run risks only if it can demonstrate other means of preventing amputations than the threat of suicide. (Kissinger, 1957, p. 135 )

Later, Fred Iklé articulated well the case against embracing mutual assured destruction (Iklé, 1973). He asked whether this "strategy" was moral or immoral, stable or intolerable. In a scathing criticism of assured destruction, he noted the convenient abstractness of referring to it: "Thus, 'assured destruction' fails to indicate what is to be destroyed, but then 'assured genocide' would reveal the truth too starkly." Iklé and many others, then, saw assured destruction as immoral and potentially ineffective.[6]

### Usability of Nuclear Weapons

Cold War history tells us much about the usability of nuclear weapons. Many people might view the United States' use of such weapons in World War II as a one-time occurrence, but numerous military and civilian leaders have contemplated their use. Douglas MacArthur regretted not being allowed to use nuclear weapons against China during the Korean war.[7] Nikita Khrushchev believed passionately in the need to avoid nuclear war but accepted that war might occur and that the Soviet Union would do whatever it took to survive and prevail (Khrushchev, 2007). In his memoirs, he also confirmed that Fidel Castro had urged Soviet use of nuclear weapons if the United States invaded Cuba. Richard Nixon claimed to be willing to use nuclear weapons in Vietnam (Gavin, 2012, p. 116). Some senior leaders of

---

[6] See Butler (2016b), which contains the memoirs of the first commander of U.S. Strategic Command, who later favored abolishing nuclear weapons.

[7] In an interview with author Bob Considine, MacArthur described the campaign against China that he was not permitted to launch, stating, "I would have dropped between 30 to 50 tactical atomic bombs on his air bases and other depots" ("Text of Accounts by Lucas and Considine in Interviews with MacArthur in 1954," 1964).

Pakistan and India have conveyed willingness to use nuclear weapons. They know that manifesting that willingness is part of deterrence (Narang, 2014).

### Credibility

One theme from Cold War deterrence theory is the crucial role of credibility. Nuclear capability and assured-retaliation capability are not enough to deter an adversary. Another necessity is the will to use the weapons if necessary. The battle of wills has long been recognized as fundamental in nuclear strategy (Schelling, 1960). According to President John F. Kennedy's National Security Advisor McGeorge Bundy, a memorandum that nuclear strategist Thomas Schelling sent to Kennedy in 1961 made a "deep impression." It stated that

> the role of nuclears in Europe should not be to win a grand nuclear campaign, but to pose a higher level of risk to the enemy. . . . The important thing in limited nuclear war is to impress the Soviet leadership with the risk of general war—a war that may occur whether we or they intend it or not. . . . We should plan for a war of nerve, of demonstration, and of bargaining, not of tactical target destruction. (Bundy, 1993, pp. 170–171)

### Enduring Issues and Schisms

Nuclear strategy, then, was discussed and debated extensively during the Cold War. Perhaps the most important conclusion was that, even in the nuclear era, war is not binary (yes, there is war; no, there is no war). Rather, wars can be large or small, targets can be discriminate or indiscriminate, and there might or might not be a winner. These complexities give rise to the concepts of levels of conflict, escalation ladders, and escalation dominance as discussed early by Herman Kahn (Kahn, 1960). These concepts, in turn, lead to arguments about the need for limited military options—and even limited nuclear options—for deterrence.

Disagreements among nuclear strategists abounded for decades and continue to exist. Table 2.1 summarizes contrasting views dating back to the early Cold War. With our apologies, the categorizations

**Table 2.1**
**Stereotypical Contrasts: How Hawks and Doves View Nuclear Issues**

| Issue | Hawks | Doves |
|---|---|---|
| Essence of deterrence | Ability to defeat any aggression | Credible threat of assured retaliatory destruction |
| Mutual assured destruction | A condition currently, but not a good one | Both a condition and the essence of nuclear strategy |
| Force requirements | Enough to defeat the opponent's attack and, where meaningful, win the subsequent war | No more than a few hundred weapons for second-strike assured destruction |
| Stringency of force requirements | Sufficient to defeat the most warfighting-oriented opponent, according to the criteria used by that opponent | No more than a few hundred weapons for second-strike assured destruction |
| Concern about opponent mindset | High: Opponent is unpredictable, might not be rational, and might even believe in winning nuclear wars (especially limited nuclear wars) | Relatively sanguine that deterrence will work |
| Doctrine | Assured retaliation, including second-strike counterforce, some first-strike counterforce, and manifest prowess | Assured destruction with modest capabilities for other functions |
| Objectives if deterrence fails | Defeat opponent's strategy and limit damage as feasible | Destroy opponent's society |
| Targeting | Military and leadership targets with countervalue attacks as only a conceivable last resort | Countervalue |
| Opponent's second-strike capability | Grudging toleration and expectation | Approval (in belief that opponent will feel secure and exhibit related self-restraint) |
| Limited war | A major concern requiring the ability to defeat aggression at many levels | Some concern but with less-stringent force requirements supplemented by inherent risk of escalation |
| Escalation dominance | Desirable and something the opponent must not have | A questionable concept |

**Table 2.1—Continued**

| Issue | Hawks | Doves |
|---|---|---|
| Relative emphasis | Deterring aggression generally with less concern about crisis stability and arms-race stability | Deterring aggression, crisis stability, and arms-race stability |
| Counterforce capability | Essential for morality and effectiveness | To be avoided except for second strike, if even then, because having such options encourages the mistaken (in this view) notion that nuclear wars can be fought and won |
| First-strike counterforce capability | Desirable, but not feasible if the opponent is sensible | Anathema |
| Strategic defenses | Desirable | Undesirable and counterproductive |
| Optimism about progress in human thinking and behavior | Minimal | Considerable |
| War with major opponent | Possible, not inevitable | Possible, not inevitable or likely |
| Arms control | Plausibly useful but to be viewed with skepticism | Strongly desirable but to be approached cautiously |
| Nuclear disarmament | No; reductions from Cold War levels were reasonable, but eliminating nuclear weapons worldwide (the goal of the "Nuclear Zero" movement) is a terrible idea | Yes |

in the table rely on stereotyping viewpoints to sharpen the contrasts. Many strategists straddle the views, sometimes inconsistently because of context. These strategists aspire to be "owls" in the "hawk" versus "dove" symbolism of war debates.

### *Counterforce*

No Cold War issue was more controversial than that of *counterforce*—targeting an enemy's nuclear forces and associated command and control for destruction. Despite impressions to the contrary, *both* sides pursued counterforce capabilities throughout the Cold War. The reasons and strategy were more subtle than is commonly appreciated.

Throughout the period, the United States continued to pursue *limited* counterforce. It rejected mutual assured destruction theory and simple-minded notions of deterrence, but it restricted itself with respect to counterforce. The culmination of this was the *countervailing strategy* announced in 1980, the result of a decade of studies across three administrations and two political parties (Slocombe, 1981). The strategy reflected the conclusion that the United States must be able to deter whoever might be leading the Soviet Union, whether a "reasonable" political leader who regarded nuclear war as altogether unacceptable or a more zealous leader convinced that, if war was necessary, it must be fought and won using military-technical criteria for assessing victory. The term *countervailing* was apt because the United States did not harbor notions of fighting and winning a nuclear war—something often misunderstood in the academic literature, as pointed out by Harold Brown (2012).

For most of the 1980s, the Soviets pursued counterforce strategy as a normal matter of course, something natural to military thinking, even though its political leaders comprehended the realities of the nuclear era. In the late 1980s, Soviet leadership came to recognize that its military doctrine was counterproductively perceived as aggressive. It began a process of deemphasizing fighting and winning wars. However, by then, the Soviet era was on its last legs. The changes that the Soviets began were little noticed in the West and proceeded to only a limited degree (Garthoff, 1992).

Perceptions on these matters were often diametrically opposite from reality, with both sides' perceptions driven by their own cultures and self-propaganda and by natural psychological foibles, such as motivational bias. Many U.S. strategists were alarmed by what they saw as an aggressive Soviet Union with leaders who believed that it was possible to fight and win a nuclear war. Halfway across the globe, Soviet leaders feared attack by an aggressive NATO. In retrospect, with the benefit of personal testimony from both sides' leaders after the Cold War, it is evident that both sides' nuclear programs were undertaken with defensive motivations (Savranskaya and Welch, 1995).

A remarkable irony about this period is that the primary Soviet military book on nuclear matters (Sokolovsky, 1984) was interpreted with alarmism by most U.S. readers but was better understood as an excellent manifestation of the Soviet leaders attempting to deter the United States (Leites, 1992). Despite claims to the contrary (including the common assertion by alleged Soviet experts that the Soviets did not even have a word for the concept), the Soviets understood deterrence. To be sure, *mutual* deterrence was not as widely accepted as desirable by the Soviets, but they certainly understood it.

During the 1970s, domestic politics became an increasingly important factor in discussions of nuclear strategy. It became an imperative in the early 1970s to assure *perceived strategic equivalence* (as distinct from inferiority).[8] That translated into requiring more U.S. counterforce capability than might otherwise have been sought. In the Soviet Union, domestic politics were less of a consideration, but—unbeknownst to Americans—the influence of its military-industrial complex had major consequences for Soviet planning, according to interviews during a window of time when such discussions were possible (Hines, Mishulovich, and Shulle, 1995). The complex affected the number of weapon-system developments, as well as the number of weapons churned out by its industry.

### *Strategic Competitiveness*

Another important development during the Cold War was the concept of *strategic competitiveness*, based on early work by Andrew Marshall (1972).[9] This concept can be seen as a supplement to deterrence-focused

[8] The imperative was a recognition of how troublesome perceived capability gaps can be in domestic political debate, even when the gaps are largely bogus (e.g., the Missile Gap asserted by Democrats in the 1960 election or the Window of Vulnerability asserted by Republicans in the 1980 election).

[9] For an interesting hagiography, see Krepinevich and Watts, 2015; for a deeper discussion, see Mahnken, 2012.

evaluation of strategy. Its intent is to win in a competition with a long-term adversary, even if the sides are adequately deterred by the threat of massive retaliation. In the Cold War, advocates of this approach argued for U.S. advances in accuracy, stealth, and networking, for both conventional and nuclear systems. In particular, stealth systems would impose large costs on the Soviet Union by rendering obsolete its then-existing air defense system. U.S. attack submarines could also pose a threat to Soviet nuclear-submarine retaliatory forces. We mention the approach here as part of reviewing lessons from the Cold War experience. For actual planners, U.S. strategy was about much more than just enhancing deterrence. That said, strategic competitiveness is not the focus of this report.

### The 1983 War Scare

A dramatic Cold War episode, now known as the "War Scare," unfolded in 1983. It started during the early Ronald Reagan administration, which was concerned about the Soviet threat and believed, based on much evidence now available but previously Top Secret (Director of Central Intelligence, 1976), that the Soviets believed that nuclear war could be fought and won. Deterring the Soviets would require disabusing them of this idea. The United States and NATO began to ratchet up the seriousness of military exercises, including for nuclear actions. According to Paul Bracken, a direct observer of the activities, a unique exercise called Proud Prophet was conducted in an intensive two-week period with senior policymakers, such as then–Secretary of Defense Casper Weinberger and then–Chairman of the Joint Chiefs of Staff John Vessey, engaged with extreme secrecy "behind the curtains" (Bracken, 2012, p. 84). Details of the exercise are not yet available publicly, but results were apparently quite sobering to officials because so many of the ideas for U.S. and NATO action were seen as irresponsible or incompatible with current U.S. capabilities when considered seriously (p. 87).

Later the same year, NATO's 1983 Able Archer exercise was also upsetting. It ended in general nuclear war with an estimated 500 million people killed just in the initial exchanges (Bracken, 2012, p. 88). In Bracken's view, the catastrophe occurred because, in a nutshell, existing strategy was faithfully followed out; forces did what they were trained to do. In the later years of the Reagan administration, senior leaders subsequently shifted gears and focused on conventional forces and following a long-term competitive strategy (p. 89).[10]

What was not recognized at the time was that U.S. and NATO behavior was quite frightening to the Soviets, whose leader (the ailing Yuri Andropov) was apparently worried or even paranoid about NATO attacking the Soviet Union. The Soviet High Command was worried that NATO might even be using Able Archer as a cover to launch a general nuclear war. They raised alert levels of some forces accordingly (President's Foreign Intelligence Advisory Board, 1990). Later, after direct discussions with Soviet leaders, President Reagan was shocked to learn of such fears. He candidly and prominently discussed this in his memoir:

> Many of us took it for granted that the Russians, like ourselves, considered it unthinkable that the United States would launch a first strike against them. But the more experience I had with the Soviet leaders and other heads of state who knew them, the more I began to realize that many Soviet officials feared us not only as adversaries but as potential aggressors who might hurl nuclear weapons at them in a first strike; because of this, and perhaps because of a sense of insecurity and paranoia with roots reaching back to the invasions of Russia by Napoleon and Hitler, they had aimed a huge arsenal of nuclear weapons at us. (Reagan, 1990)

U.S. intelligence officers and some high-ranking officials initially doubted Soviet fears, but a later report (originally Top Secret) con-

---

[10] Additional previously classified information on nuclear matters continues to emerge (Burr, 2016). The differences between policy and practice through most of the 1980s are discussed with anguish by retired GEN George (Lee) Butler in his memoirs (Butler, 2016a; Butler, 2016b). Among the revelations is that, despite years of presidential directives, many options sought by policymakers were still not available operationally. For example, as of the early 1980s, *city withholds* (not targeting civilian populations in cities) were not realistically available. Also, a *launch under attack* capability (launching retaliatory forces on confirmed warning of an underway attack) was effectively automatic. Such problems were reportedly fixed by the late 1980s but only after extraordinary efforts over many years (see Franklin Miller's contributions to Butler, 2016b, Chapter 23).

cluded that the concerns were real and that U.S. assessments had been wrong (President's Foreign Intelligence Advisory Board, 1990). Arguably, NATO's efforts to improve deterrence succeeded—but at a high price to crisis stability.

## Lessons Learned, Valid and Invalid

### Disagreements

One view of lessons learned is that (1) limited nuclear options are a fraud because, in reality, the opponent would probably react massively, and (2) military leaders choose for their actions and plans not to be as subtle and distinction-making as those of armchair strategists. This set of lessons is sometimes drawn from observation of military practice in both NATO and the Warsaw Pact and from the discouraging results of exercises and games in the early 1980s (see the previous section).

An alternative view is that, in the event of *real* crisis, policymakers in the primary countries would go to extraordinary lengths to control escalation rather than begin the process of mutual suicide. In this view, the actual war plans and the games and exercises were not nearly as real as they seemed to be, and they proved nothing. The Able Archer exercise in 1983, for example, demonstrated consequences of the sides implementing their plans and doctrine. But in an actual crisis and conflict, wiser heads might have prevailed and—despite problems of command, control, communications, and execution—total catastrophe might have been averted.

The contradictions exist, in part, because governments chose to pursue ambiguous strategies. On the one hand, deterrence was served by elevating fear that war would escalate to general nuclear war. On the other hand, the belief was that deterrence of some actors in some circumstances would be served by being capable and credible about using nuclear weapons on a limited basis. We do not see any way to declare one or the other to be correct, based on historical experience. We see the first set of lessons to be profound cautions but not decisively predictive.

### What U.S. Governments Concluded About Nuclear Deterrence

In looking at the documentary record, we can make several observations about what past U.S. governments have decided on nuclear matters. First, preparing for *assured retaliation*—that is, assured second-strike capability—was paramount from the 1970s onward. Significantly, however, the notion of assured retaliatory "destruction" had largely disappeared by the 1970s. The criteria of sufficiency were stringent, but not in terms of killing people. It was deemed necessary for a second strike to be able to destroy thousands of military, political, and economic targets even after the United States suffered a surprise first strike. Despite the rhetoric of some of former U.S. Secretary of Defense Robert McNamara's earlier public speeches, the targeting of cities per se was to be abhorred except as a last resort.[11] Higher priority was placed on military targets and, by 1980, the destruction of the Soviet political control structure. The United States maintained substantial counterforce capability against nuclear delivery systems and broader countermilitary capability against, for example, military bases and other installations. Since the late 1970s, there has been relatively more emphasis on second-strike counterforce that would deny the Soviets a postexchange advantage without threatening a disarming first-strike capability, but the United States has consistently maintained a significant degree of first-strike counterforce as well. This is partly a result of U.S. leaders accepting, to some degree, tenets of the strategic-competition school, to include assuring no less than perceived strategic equivalence, imposing costs on the Soviets (e.g., stealth technology rendered earlier air and missile defenses obsolete), and demonstrating technological superiority.

Although achieving deterrence by threat of assured retaliation has been paramount, the U.S. government has always recognized the objective of limiting damage if deterrence fails. The extremely limited efforts in strategic defense and civil defense were due to technical difficulties, economics, and lack of domestic enthusiasm, not philosophical

---

[11] That intention of Defense Secretaries and Presidents would not be achieved in operational targeting plans until the late 1980s (Butler, 2016b)—many years after the policy directives.

condemnation (as evidenced by the temporary re-ascendance of strategic defense under President Reagan).

At no time after the 1950s was it believed that the threat of mutual assured destruction was sufficient to deter limited aggression. That is, the concept of minimum deterrence has been repeatedly rejected when carefully examined.[12]

Some additional lessons from the Cold War come from Bracken (2012). He notes that nuclear weapons are often used without firing them and that countries play nuclear "head games," brandishing nuclear weapons in attempts to influence others. In all such instances, both individuals and institutions influence what happens. Because of all this complexity, it is easy for leaders to misunderstand or miscalculate risks.

### Decisions About Nonstrategic Nuclear Weapons

The literature is much less rich on the Cold War history of government leaders' attitudes about tactical and theater-nuclear weapons than it is on their attitudes about strategic weapons, but several points can be made (Cimbala, 2018, pp. 169–191).

Much confusion results from the lack of precise definitions for many of the categories used in discourse about NSNW and limited use. *Strategic* nuclear delivery systems are defined by the New Strategic Arms Reduction Treaty (START) as those with ranges greater than 5,500 km (approximately the distance between the United States and Russia) (United States and Russia, 2010). All other nuclear delivery systems are therefore *nonstrategic* or *substrategic*, irrespective of the yields of the warheads they carry or their anticipated targets. The Intermediate-Range Nuclear Forces Treaty bans all nuclear-capable land-based missiles with ranges between 500 and 5,500 km (United States and Soviet Union, 1987). Air-launched missiles, such as the Russian Kh-102 and U.S. AGM-86 air-launched cruise missile (ALCM),

---

[12] The issue has been fiercely debated over the years, but the George W. Bush, Barack Obama, and Donald Trump administrations have continued to include counterforce capabilities and to reject minimum deterrence in their nuclear policies (U.S. Department of State, 2016; Roberts, 2015; DoD, 2018). Minimum deterrence also requires adherence to the principles of the Law of Armed Conflict.

are usually regarded as strategic weapons even though they can deliver low-yield warheads and the missiles and aircraft that carry them can operate at substrategic ranges. The English-language term *tactical nuclear weapons* was used during the Cold War to refer to short-range battlefield nuclear weapons intended to be used at the front of the battle (where contact occurs) to achieve tactical objectives rather than in the rear (to the extent that such distinctions are meaningful in a nuclear war). Today, the term is sometimes employed casually to refer to all NSNW, particularly those with low yields. Official documents are more careful on the matter.

### Purpose

Although both sides' armies retained the capability for battlefield nuclear use throughout the Cold War, they primarily focused their army efforts on conventional conflict. The United States had attempted major reorganization of the U.S. Army for the nuclear battlefield in the 1950s (the Pentomic division) but had encountered fundamental difficulties relating to command and control, the likelihood of massive civilian casualties even when nuclear war was "limited," and the early conclusion that battlefield use did not even favor the defense.[13] The United States moved away from notions of battlefield nuclear war by instead emphasizing the deterrent value of a broad *flexible response* approach that could involve diplomatic and economic measures, limited military measures, unconventional military measures (e.g., use of special forces), and so forth. The flexible response approach included use of *limited nuclear options* and was seen as a contrast to planning to fight and win a tactical nuclear war.

Ideas and capabilities for such limited options evolved a good deal in the 1960s during the Kennedy and Lyndon B. Johnson administrations, building on ideas and capabilities from the late 1950s. Battlefield nuclear weapons continued to be part of the arsenal, doctrine, and training, but it was commonly believed that they should be used only

[13] This refers to the outcome of the earlier 1955 exercise called Sagebrush, held in Louisiana to simulate atomic war. Some of the problems observed were overcome technically in later years, but the attitude about the hopelessness of effective battlefield use continued.

in desperation when conventional defense was failing. The prospect of using limited nuclear options, it was hoped, would enhance deterrence.[14] Some others had ambitions for more-effective use, to include blunting Soviet invasion to create the opportunity for war termination on terms acceptable to NATO.[15] Actual developments were not conspicuously coherent. Somewhat later, technological developments made possible more militarily effective weapons with reduced collateral damage (e.g., the enhanced-radiation weapons, also called neutron bombs, debated in the late 1970s). Public opinion and political pressures led President Jimmy Carter to delay the enhanced-radiation weapon program indefinitely, although he secretly ordered production of components (Nichols, Stuart, and McCausland, 2012, pp. ix, 50).

### Targeting

By 1986, NATO's Nuclear Planning Group approved important guidelines stating that "initial use of nuclear weapons would occur mainly on the territory of the aggressor" (Nichols, Stuart, and McCausland, 2012, p. 56).[16] Furthermore, "the principal purpose would be to signal NATO resolve to escalate to the strategic level if necessary. The guidelines shifted the weight of targeting options from the battlefield toward deep strikes on Warsaw Pact territory" (p. 56). The shift, then, was toward signaling and away from warfighting, but the planning was to cover every contingency and rule out none.

The natural inclination is to draw the lesson that, based on Cold War experience, NSNW or tactical nuclear weapons should, in the context of deterrence, be seen more for their symbolic roles in raising

---

[14] See Nichols, Stuart, and McCausland, 2012, p. ix. As Paul Schulte mentions later in the same book, the significance of tactical nuclear weapons has varied with context (Schulte, 2012, pp. 16–33).

[15] Former U.S. Secretary of Defense James Schlesinger hoped for a major rethinking that would lead to more-coherent strategy, forces, and posturing. A recently declassified report gives a thorough discussion (Schlesinger, 1975).

[16] The Nuclear Planning Group acts as NATO's senior body on nuclear matters and reviews the Alliance's nuclear policy in light of the ever-changing security environment. It consists of *all* NATO member states, with the exception of France, which has decided not to participate. It is chaired by the Secretary General of NATO.

stakes and increasing fears about general nuclear war than for their military effectiveness on the battlefield. Drawing that conclusion, however, would be to rely unduly on the NATO-Soviet experience. Since the Cold War, additional nations, such as Pakistan and India, have developed nuclear weapons and thought about their operational value in addition to their deterrence capability (Tellis, Fair, and Medby, 2001). Mansoor Ahmed, for example, addresses Pakistani operational issues (Ahmed, 2016). Another source of post–Cold War thinking (Frankel, Scouras, and Ullrich, 2017) reviews issues for NATO as seen in 2012. That report notes that Russia has developed modern-technology nuclear options that could enhance effectiveness and usability. These appear similar to the enhanced-radiation weapons contemplated by NATO in the 1970s (see also Chapter Three).

CHAPTER THREE

# Developments Since the Cold War

Many geostrategic changes have occurred since the Cold War that bear on nuclear forces (Bracken, 2012; National Research Council, 2014, p. 27; Roberts, 2015; DoD, 2018). One change is not always recognized. In the Cold War, there were few *objective* reasons for direct clashes between the United States and the Soviet Union, or even between NATO and the Soviet Union. Both sides planned for defending against aggression and postulated corresponding scenarios (as discussed in Chapter Two), but neither actually had intentions for war (Morgan, 2003) and both sides were cautious. Even Kahn regarded the United States and Soviet Union as status-quo powers (Kahn, 1960).

Since the Cold War, particularly under President Vladimir Putin, Russia has been anguished by the status quo, angry with and fearful of NATO, and desirous of reestablishing aspects of the previous order. Russia is revisionist (Johnson, 2018), as illustrated by its annexation of Crimea in 2014. Russia will probably continue to seek favorable revisions in the security environment through aggressive means, but means that are intended to avoid war with NATO. Russia has given considerable thought to the subtleties of conflict by nonmilitary means, including the peacetime and crisis roles of information warfare and what Westerners refer to as gray-zone or hybrid-warfare methods (Chivvis, 2017; Johnson, 2018).

We touch here on only some aspects of change, focusing on NSNW. First, we discuss Russia's developments and then NATO's developments. After that, we discuss some particular problems that NATO faces.

## Developments in Russian Strategy and Nuclear Weapons Within It

### Russian Thinking About Classes of War

Russian strategic thinking distinguishes among local, regional, and large-scale (*krupnomasshtabnaia*) (Ministry of Defence of the Russian Federation, undated). *Local* conflicts are fought by limited forces and without the use of nuclear weapons. *Regional* conflicts are fought by two or more states in a region with national or coalition forces. Such conflicts could grow out of local wars or escalating crises; they might include use of nuclear weapons. *Large-scale* wars transcend regions; they could include general nuclear war, although Russia recognizes that outcome as an ultimate disaster to be avoided. NSNW are implicitly intended for threatened or actual use in regional wars (Johnson, 2018; Durkalec, 2015, 2018).

Today, Russia regards nuclear weapons as a core element of its ability to deter China and NATO from nuclear or conventional attack and has many potential options for using such weapons on the battlefield and geostrategically for escalation control or military effect. The 2014 version of the Military Doctrine of the Russian Federation states,

> the Russian Federation reserves the right to use nuclear weapons in response to the utilization of nuclear and other types of weapons of mass destruction against it and (or) its allies and also in the event of aggression against the Russian Federation involving the use of conventional weapons when the very existence of the state is in jeopardy. (President of the Russian Federation, 2014, para. 27)

President Putin quoted this doctrine in a recent speech introducing new nuclear delivery systems, characterizing it approvingly as "concise, clear, and concrete" (Putin, 2018).

### Russia's Theory of Victory

Former DoD official Brad Roberts argues that Russia has a theory of victory regarding a regional war with NATO:

> Moscow hopes to achieve its operational and political objectives quickly at the conventional level while having credible capabili-

> ties to manage the risks of escalation against a conventionally superior, nuclear-armed alliance. Such as it can be derived from available official statements and literature and associated analysis . . . the Russian theory apparently begins with an effort to create a military fait accompli on the ground. . . . The Russian theory . . . also includes a significant dimension related to countering possible escalatory responses by the United States and NATO. Russia has developed both horizontal and vertical options to counter and disincentivize Western escalation. Horizontal escalation would encompass standoff strikes on targets beyond the immediate zone of hybrid combat but within the "strategic direction." Vertical escalation would encompass strikes by both nuclear and nonnuclear means (whether kinetic or nonkinetic).
>
> . . . Nonstrategic nuclear weapons apparently play a central role. . . . Actual employment would apparently be preemptive in nature and intended to deescalate a conflict. Presumably this follows from the calculus of Russian leadership that their employment of nuclear weapons against NATO forces would signal their resolve and alert Western decision makers to the asymmetry of stakes, as Russian leaders perceive it. . . . Some Russians have also described an effort to calibrate the amount of "tailored damage" that would be needed to induce the desired restraint by NATO rather than inciting it to further action. (Roberts, 2015, pp. 133–134)

### When Might Russia Employ Nonstrategic Nuclear Weapons?

When, more concretely, might Russia use nuclear weapons? From the Russian military perspective, the answer might be as described in an article in the Russian journal of military thought *Voennaya Mysl'* (Aksenov, Tret'yakov, and Filin, 2015). Beyond the obvious case of retaliation to enemy nuclear attack, the circumstances might include

- the certain discovery of direct intention by the adversary for nuclear weapon employment
- the adversary's use of conventional weapons against strategically important targets
- the threat of the adversary's mass strike by precision weapons

- degradation of Russia's defense capacity to critical (unacceptable) levels during the nonnuclear phase of conflict.

Although such listings are always ambiguous, there is considerable reason to believe that Russia sees its integrated air defense systems (IADSs) in the western part of the country as strategically important and as something that cannot be allowed to degrade to unacceptable levels. Thus, a lively debate has emerged in the Russian military press about whether—in the event of regional war with NATO—Russia should attempt to preempt such threats by attacking first (Velez-Green, 2018).

For U.S. and NATO strategists, it would seem that Russian doctrine would notably apply to a scenario of Russian aggression, such as a Russian invasion of the Baltic states that quickly suffered conventional reverses or looked as though it might be followed by a major NATO military response that would bring to bear NATO's overall military and economic strength, perhaps over many months or a few years.[1] In either circumstance, logic suggests that Moscow might try to salvage the situation by using nuclear escalation to achieve war termination (de-escalation) *on conditions favorable to Russia*. Such a Russian escalation is sometimes envisioned as a tactical strike on NATO conventional forces in the Baltic states (Krepinevich and Cohn, 2016) or a *demonstration strike* that results in few or no direct casualties (Luik and Jermalavičius, 2017). Other analysts contend that Russia might even employ a demonstration strike early in a Baltic conflict, before it begins suffering conventional reverses, to intimidate NATO governments and consolidate its gains.

### Purpose of Russian Nonstrategic Nuclear Weapon Systems

Russia's post-Soviet nuclear forces seek to enable two aims: providing an assured retaliation capability and enabling selective options with either

1 The possibility of a Russian invasion of the Baltic states that quickly suffered conventional reverses was more plausible to Russians when the concept of *escalate to de-escalate* was first announced in 2000 because of NATO's great superiority at the time in long-range precision weapons (Sokov, 2014). As noted elsewhere, initial versions were reminiscent of NATO's use of flexible response in the Cold War to offset its conventional-warfare disadvantages (Zysk, 2017).

strategic or substrategic systems. One Russian analyst characterized his country's nuclear strategy as combining a mutual assured destruction capability with limited warfighting (Pechatnov, 2010). Russian thinkers have engaged in many debates about the purpose and use of Russia's substantial nuclear capabilities, which are broad and practiced. Those capabilities could be used for small demonstration strikes; small, for-effect strikes; and larger uses, all of which NATO needs to consider.

Until the 2010s, many analysts assumed that Russia was holding on to its NSNW because they represented a low-cost, high-leverage element for negotiations about, for example, arms control or NATO's ballistic-missile deployment in Europe. That view became untenable as Russia introduced new nuclear-capable theater delivery systems and spoke more openly about their potential nuclear delivery role.

It is of interest that none of the publicly announced systems is a battlefield weapon, such as a nuclear artillery shell.[2] Instead, these are such systems as the operational-tactical Iskander-M missile (less than a 500-km range) and the longer-range Novator 9M720 ground-launched cruise missile (GLCM) and air-launched hypersonic Kinzhal Kh-47M2. The logical application of these weapons in a conflict with NATO would be to strike targets in Central and Western Europe, rather than in the Baltic states, with either precision conventional or nuclear warheads.[3]

If doubt exists about the seriousness of Russian intentions for the use of nuclear weapons, the past decade's exercises should dispel it (see, for example, Schneider, 2017).

---

2 Early in the 21st century, Russia announced retirement of warheads for the Russian Ground Forces, including nuclear artillery and nuclear warheads for tactical missiles (Sokov, 2012). More recently, Russia has not stated that the ground forces still lack nuclear weapons, so a reversal may have occurred (e.g., for Iskander missiles with nuclear weapons). In any case, Russian Ground Forces still train for nuclear war with well-equipped and integrated nuclear, biological, and chemical defense units, even though Russians would prefer to use combinations of precision weapons to achieve comparable objectives without the hazards of nuclear employment (Grau and Bartles, 2017).

3 Some have argued that these systems are primarily for delivery of precision conventional munitions (Tetrais, 2018), but their small number suggests that they will have a substantially or primarily nuclear role for the foreseeable future.

### Western Debates About What the Russian Strategy Is

It is broadly accepted that Russia has developed plans, capabilities, and doctrine for coercive use of NSNW to bring about war termination on circumstances favorable to Russia. There is, however, a great deal of debate about details—in particular, whether NSNW employment would be an exercise in brinkmanship and stakes-raising, an exercise with decisive military elements, or both. Also, scholarly debate exists on whether Russian employment would be (1) discriminate, focused on the use of small-yield weapons and minimizing collateral damage, or (2) governed by purely military considerations.

Debate in the West is due largely to authors seeing various aspects of vigorous debate within Russia. We touch on various elements of this interesting but confusing discussion in what follows, but, in a sense, it is a diversion. Ultimately, we see it as crucial to recognize two things: First, Russian strategists recognize all the same subtleties, dilemmas, and cases that Americans do. Second, Russia has the *capability* to tailor nuclear use as needed at the time, whether such use be demonstrative (symbolic) or militarily effective and whether it be very limited and discriminate, very limited but not so discriminate, or less limited and less discriminate.

When contemplating deterrence capabilities and options to improve them, we should test the concepts by recognizing that Russia might simply make a wise decision when the time comes to decide how to act. Ultimately, a best estimate of how Russian planners think about such matters today, in the abstract, is not very useful.[4] Intentions change, and circumstances can vary.[5] With that preface, the following sections highlight the available literature on these various debates.

---

[4] This is a special case of a broader principle: Strategy should be designed for flexibility, adaptiveness, and robustness, not for a particular case, even an allegedly best-estimate case. A considerable literature exists on the matter, extending from defense planning (for a review, see Davis, 2014) to a wide range of social-policy issues (see pointers to the literature at RAND Corporation, undated).

[5] For examples of subtle Russian thinking on matters of nuclear deterrence, see Sokov, 2004.

### *Declaratory Policy Versus Employment Policy*

It is important to distinguish between *declaratory policy*, which exists to signal to adversaries and allies, and *employment policy* (or *action policy*), which characterizes how and when weapons would actually be employed. Declaratory policy has to be public. Official statements, such as comments by Putin, are signaling. Sometimes, they can suggest that the threshold for using nuclear weapons is lower than it actually is—so as to increase the credibility of deterrent threats. Putin used nuclear signaling during the Ukrainian crisis in 2014 (Durkalec, 2015). Other times, Putin's statements are intended to suggest strength, maturity, and sobriety (Oliker and Baklitskiy, 2018).

Employment policy, meanwhile, tends to be shrouded in secrecy. To be sure, it is constrained by military hardware and institutional practices, some of which can be inferred by observation of weapons deployments and training regimes. In any case, when drawing on the open Russian literature, we should be aware that only some of the authors know what actual employment policy is, or even the inside rationale for declaratory policy. Some publications may even contradict actual Russian policies and may be part of internal Russian debate about what policies should be. It is for these and other reasons that Olga Oliker has observed that "Russian nuclear strategy is not obvious" (Oliker, 2016).

### *Russian Limited-Use Strategy*

The view that Russia's nuclear arsenal is designed to enable brinkmanship and coercion has become increasingly influential in recent years and, in 2015, was made an official assumption in the formulation of U.S. defense policy when DoD officials testified that

> Russian military doctrine includes what some have called an "escalate to de-escalate" strategy—a strategy that purportedly seeks to de-escalate a conventional conflict through coercive threats, including limited nuclear use. (Work and Winnefeld, 2015)

Similarly, the 2018 Nuclear Posture Review asserts that

> Russia's national security policies, strategy, and doctrine . . . include an emphasis on the threat of limited nuclear escalation

> and that Moscow threatens and exercises limited nuclear first use, suggesting a mistaken expectation that coercive nuclear threats or limited first use could paralyze the United States and NATO and thereby end a conflict on terms favorable to Russia. (DoD, 2018)

But what does *escalate to de-escalate* mean?

The DoD statements just noted do not describe what limited Russian escalation would look like in detail, but much discussion ascribes to it a political character associated with brinkmanship and stakes-raising, as in the Cold War literature. For example, Miller (2018) states, "The Russian military has devised a doctrine which envisions using a small number of very low-yield nuclear weapons to attack NATO forces defending Alliance territory." Elbridge Colby of the Center for a New American Security notes, "the purpose of such strikes would not, presumably, be to defeat the alliance's military or strategic forces outright, but rather to manipulate the risk of escalation in such a way that Moscow would come out of the contest of wills the victor" (Colby, 2016).[6] And Katarzyna Zysk notes, "The primary objective of limited nuclear use would be political: to coerce the adversary to cease aggression through a demonstration of Russia's determination and readiness to bring hostilities to a halt" (Zysk, 2018).[7]

This conception of de-escalation implicitly discounts the possibility that Russia could employ theater-nuclear strikes to blunt or eliminate NATO's ability to sustain military operations against Moscow. That is, the concept discounts that Russia's NSNW could be employed for decisive military effect and that Russian leaders might be willing to accept considerable collateral damage to achieve such effect. Indeed, some analysts have argued that Russian NSNW are intended for war-

[6] Elsewhere in the article, Colby acknowledges that a much wider range of strikes is possible.

[7] This interpretation of Russian strategy is elaborated in the richly cited Zysk, 2017. Zysk states that this feature of Russian military strategy has been corroborated by strategic documents, official statements, programs, deployments, and operations. We find, however, that the Russian document cited in Zysk (2018) to support this contention (President of the Russian Federation, 2017) does not discuss objectives of limited nuclear use or mention NSNW. Our reading of the same literature does not convince us that demonstration uses are the most likely form that Russian limited nuclear use would take.

fighting purposes rather than as deterrence instruments (Blank, 2011). Certainly, the Russian military develops weapons for military purposes. As Russian scholar (and former Deputy Chairman of the Duma Defense Committee) Alexei Arbatov has noted,

> in the 70-year history of nuclear weapons never has a single system or single unit been created or accepted into the arsenal for the abstract aim of deterrence. These means have always been created and developed for fulfilment of concrete combat goals and destruction of specific targets in accordance with real operational plans for the conduct of nuclear war. (Arbatov, 2014, in Russian; also cited in Johnson, 2016, p. 43)

Former Soviet and Russian Foreign Ministry official Nikolai Sokov (now at the Middlebury Institute) concluded in 2012 that "Russian 'de-escalation' strategy foresees limited use of nuclear weapons against bases, aircraft carriers, and command and control centers" that would be used to launch precision-guided munitions into Russia (Sokov, 2012). It is also interesting to note that Russian military exercises over the past decade have apparently demonstrated (or simulated) the capability for everything from small and discriminate to large and indiscriminate nuclear use (Schneider, 2017), although some exercises have reportedly and notably lacked a nuclear component (Oliker and Baklitskiy, 2018).

### *Origins of the Phrase* Escalate to De-Escalate

The phrase *escalate to de-escalate* is Western usage, not Russian. It originated in English-language discussions of Russian strategic writings; Russian-language sources employed a single word, *deyeskalatsiia*, which rose to prominence in the late 1990s with some much-discussed articles in military science publications (Levshin, Nedelin, and Sosnovskii, 1999).[8] The term *de-escalation of aggression* later appeared in a Russian defense-ministry white paper in 2003, but it was defined in vague

[8] The full phrase appears in Russian in discussions of Western interpretations of Russian nuclear strategy and is variously translated as "эскалация-деэскалация" or "эскалация ради деэскалация" (see, for example, Kostrzewa–Zorbas, 2016).

terms: to "forc[e] the enemy to halt military action by a threat to deliver or by actual delivery of strikes of varying intensity with reliance on conventional and/or nuclear weapons" (Sokov, 2014). *Deyeskalatsiia* is therefore not a strategy or a doctrine but rather an *objective* to be sought with strategic instruments ranging from threats to nuclear attack. The definition does not indicate what kind of Russian threats or attacks are contemplated.

As noted earlier, much of the confusion in the West about contemporary Russian nuclear strategy seems to reflect ongoing debates among Russian policy and military establishments about what the country's declaratory and action policies should be. Military journal articles about de-escalation often appear to be works of advocacy in Russia, not a Rosetta Stone for Russia's nuclear operation planning (Oliker, 2016). Proponents can be found in Russian defense discourse for an immense array of approaches to nuclear strategy, of which de-escalation after small demonstrative use is only one.

### *Low-Yield Weapons and Discriminate Use*

It is common for Western authors to conflate escalate to de-escalate actions with use of substrategic weapons that have low yields. The conflation may be because of concepts familiar in U.S. and NATO strategic cultures. Nuclear brinkmanship was much discussed in the classic works on nuclear strategy by Schelling, Kahn, and others. Moreover, many Westerners internalized the assumption that NSNW could not be used to effectively redress the military balance. This was an accurate characterization of the military situation in Europe from the 1960s until the end of the Cold War. Kahn commented,

> Almost every analyst now agrees that . . . the first use of nuclear weapons—even against military targets—is likely to be less for the purpose of destroying the other side's military targets than for "redressive, warning, bargaining, fining, or deterrence purposes." (Kahn, 1965, p. 138)

The original 1999 *Military Thought* (*Voennaya Mysl'*) article advocating de-escalation (Levshin, Nedelin, and Sosnovskii, 1999) also coincided with a moment of extreme Russian military and technological weakness. At the time, both Russian and Western analysts assumed that Russia would quickly falter in a conventional conflict with NATO. In that context, a NATO-style limited (even demonstrative) use by Russia may have made sense, especially with low-yield weapons. That prospect was probably seen as Russia making use of a tactic (flexible response with limited nuclear use as describe in Chapter Two) that NATO had employed during the Cold War. Another important source of enthusiasm for low-yield weapons was that of the Russian nuclear weapon complex, which sought to develop exotic new low-yield warheads that would produce high-energy X-rays. Advocates claimed that these weapons (which might, among other things, create greatly enhanced electromagnetic pulse effects) could offset Russian military weakness relative to NATO (Central Intelligence Agency Office of Transnational Issues, 2000).[9]

In summary, Russia has developed low-yield weapons and likely has options for employing them, but it is probably an error to assume that a Russian effort to escalate for the purpose of de-escalating (i.e., of achieving war termination on favorable terms) would be limited to low-yield weapons. It might or might not.

## NATO Developments Since the Cold War

NATO's approach to nuclear weapons has undergone complex evolution, owing to the multitude of stakeholders with divergent interests and calculations within the Alliance. Nuclear deterrence was de-emphasized in the 1990s and 2000s as NATO focused on other concerns, such as conflicts in the Balkans and Afghanistan. In the aftermath of Russia's annexation of Crimea in 2014, the Alliance began devoting increased attention to bolstering nuclear deterrence. In this section, we examine a few of these considerations and their implications for U.S. policy.

---

[9] These enhanced radiation warheads also had factors militating against them—not the least of which was that their unusual X-ray output would probably require atmospheric nuclear tests to ascertain their military effects.

Until recently, NATO's nuclear deterrence policy was based on the 2010 Strategic Concept (NATO, 2010) and the 2012 Deterrence and Defense Posture Review (NATO, 2012), agreed on by all 29 NATO allies. The following were among the themes of the Posture Review (all quotations from NATO, 2012):

1. Identify the Alliance's goals and core strategy elements, including deterrence:

   > The greatest responsibility of the Alliance is to protect and defend our territory and our populations against attack, as set out in Article 5 of the Washington Treaty. . . . Allies' goal is to bolster deterrence as a core element of our collective defence and contribute to the indivisible security of the Alliance. (para. 2)

2. Emphasize NATO's desire to remain a nuclear alliance while highlighting the role of conventional forces in deterrence:

   > Nuclear weapons are a core component of NATO's overall capabilities for deterrence and defence alongside conventional and missile defence forces. . . . As long as nuclear weapons exist, NATO will remain a nuclear alliance. (para. 8)

3. Highlight the role of strategic nuclear forces, particularly those of the United States, in deterrence:

   > The supreme guarantee of the security of the Allies is provided by the strategic nuclear forces of the Alliance, particularly those of the United States; the independent strategic nuclear forces of the United Kingdom and France, which have a deterrent role of their own, contribute to the overall deterrence and security of the Allies. (para. 9)

4. Indicate a desire for further reduction of NSNW, but signal that these would require reciprocal moves by Russia:

   > While seeking to create the conditions and considering options for further reductions of non-strategic nuclear weapons assigned

> to NATO, Allies concerned [i.e., all members of the Nuclear Planning Group] will ensure that all components of NATO's nuclear deterrent remain safe, secure, and effective for as long as NATO remains a nuclear alliance. . . . NATO is prepared to consider further reducing its requirement for non-strategic nuclear weapons assigned to the Alliance in the context of reciprocal steps by Russia, taking into account the greater Russian stockpiles of non-strategic nuclear weapons stationed in the Euro-Atlantic area. (paras. 11, 20)

5. Leave the door open for adjustments in strategy in response to a changing security environment:

> NATO will continue to adjust its strategy, including with respect to the capabilities and other measures required for deterrence and defence, in line with trends in the security environment. (para. 34)

In recent years, NATO has made significant adaptations to policy (Durkalec, 2018). For example, since 2014, allied governments have agreed on measures to revitalize the role of nuclear weapons in NATO's overall defense and deterrent posture and to enhance the survivability and operational capabilities of its nuclear forces.

After a meeting in Brussels in 2018, the summit declaration stated, in part,

> Allies' goal is to continue to bolster deterrence as a core element of our collective defence and to contribute to the indivisible security of the Alliance. Following changes in the security environment, NATO has taken steps to ensure its nuclear deterrent capabilities remain safe, secure, and effective. . . . Allies concerned will continue to take steps to ensure sustained leadership focus and institutional excellence for the nuclear deterrence mission, coherence between conventional and nuclear components of NATO's deterrence and defence posture, and effective strategic communications. (NATO, 2018b, para. 35)

The 2018 U.S. Nuclear Posture Review reflects some of these same points, noting that

> The Alliance has already initiated measures to ensure that NATO's overall deterrence and defense posture, including its nuclear forces, remain capable of addressing any potential adversary's doctrine and capabilities.
>
> In support of these efforts, the United States will consult and work cooperatively with NATO allies to:
>
> - Enhance the readiness and survivability of NATO [dual capable aircraft], improve capabilities required to increase their operational effectiveness, and account for adversary nuclear and non-nuclear capabilities;
> - Promote the broadest possible participation of Allies in their agreed burden sharing arrangements regarding the [dual capable aircraft] mission, nuclear mission support, and nuclear infrastructure;
> - Replace aging aircraft and weapons systems with modernized or life-extended equivalents as they age out;
> - Enhance the realism of training and exercise programs to ensure the Alliance can effectively integrate nuclear and non-nuclear operations, if deterrence fails; and
> - Ensure the NATO [nuclear command, control, and communications] system is modernized to enable appropriate consultations and effective nuclear operations, improve its survivability, resilience, and flexibility in the most stressful threat environments. (DoD, 2018, p. 60)

More broadly, thoughts about how NATO should adapt to deal with threats like those that Russia poses to the Baltic states have had three themes:

1. the addition of significant conventional forces in and around the Baltic states as a credible means to slow down or stop the invading Russian forces

2. the development and fielding of nuclear options, as well as joint training in their use, to enable effective employment of these classes of weapons (related options are discussed in DoD, 2018)
3. the dispersal and hardening of bases and command and control nodes throughout NATO territory to avoid presenting a small number of high-value targets to the Russians.

Advancing any of these themes would require significant peacetime investments from all allies, although the burden might be shared unevenly. In particular, the implications to European NATO member states would be as follows:

- Theme 1: The costs to European allies would exceed the costs of simply equipping and fielding units. Indeed, the infrastructure investments (e.g., airports, ports, railways, roads) required to move troops from the United States to Europe, as well as to move and logistically support troops within Europe, would be substantial and would have to be borne by European, non-Baltic NATO member states.
- Theme 2: Governments of some European NATO member states have expressed concern over the security risks, credibility, and financial and political costs of the current posture (Andreasen et al., 2018). Any further addition of NSNW in Europe, and the necessity for new investments in procuring and maintaining dual-capable aircraft, will likely give rise to similar, if not heightened, concerns. The 2018 Nuclear Posture Review postulates the employment of submarine-launched ballistic missiles (SLBMS) and submarine-launched cruise missiles (SLCMs) to minimize the reliance on host-nation support: "Unlike [dual capable aircraft], a low-yield SLBM warhead and SLCM will not require or rely on host nation support to provide deterrent effect" (DoD, 2018, p. xii). Although such options indeed require less buy-in from European host nations, submarine launches present increased challenges in communicating the intended tactical use, thereby raising the specter of unintended general nuclear war.

They may also seem to decouple U.S. decisions from NATO decisions, thereby reducing credibility of their use in Russian eyes.

- Theme 3: The dispersal of basing and command and control nodes around Europe runs directly counter to the trend toward increasing centralization since the end of the Cold War. Beyond cost considerations, continuing public sensitivity to nuclear weapons in Europe may render basing dispersal a particularly fraught endeavor. Finally, the burden to European countries is present regardless of the choice of weapons and delivery mode, whether based on the ground in Europe, delivered by dual capable aircraft, or launched by submarine (as proposed in the 2018 Nuclear Posture Review).

A June 2018 meeting at the UK government's Wilton Park agency concluded that, although NATO's recent steps are positive, they are far from sufficient to mitigate the threat from Russia. As the resulting report noted, "NATO has also not revised its operational concepts to account for the requirements of effectively countering new developments in Russian doctrine and capabilities," leading participants to conclude that, "Even in the absence of a new strategy and new operational concepts, we know enough about the challenges posed by Russian strategy and capabilities to conclude that further adaptation is essential to ensure the Alliance's deterrence credibility" (Messmer and Roberts, 2018). As we discuss in the next chapter, Russia today enjoys an in-theater asymmetry that is hard to counter—namely, the lack of Warsaw Pact countries (or their equivalent nowadays, with the possible exception of Belarus). Barring direct nuclear confrontation on U.S. and Russian soil, most nuclear exchanges would be carried out against European NATO targets or U.S. strategic assets outside the continental United States, and all nonmilitary effects (e.g., civilian casualties, destruction of infrastructure, environmental consequences) would be borne by U.S. allies and strategic partners. Thus, compared with the cost to Russia and the United States, the cost to European NATO allies would increase more rapidly with the number of NSNW employed (or as the situation reached higher rungs on the escalation ladder), owing to the mounting nonmilitary losses borne by Europe and its population.

All of these considerations raise serious questions about the likelihood of NATO allies adopting a deterrence strategy for the Baltic states predicated on U.S. nonnuclear strategic weapons (whether surface-, air-, or submarine-launched) in view of the high costs that such a strategy would impose on European NATO allies in peacetime—and particularly during and after a conflict.

## Realities of Geography and Conventional Force Balances

During the Cold War, the overall ratio of Warsaw Pact forces to NATO forces was about 1.6 to one. Nonetheless, "NATO was postured with local conventional forces sufficient to defend a contiguous line, with reserves, and with rehearsed deployments for reinforcements able to prevent a rapid *fait accompli*" (Boston et al., 2018, p. 3). In the current (as of 2018) situation in the Baltic states, NATO ground forces are substantially outnumbered (by as much as five to one) while potentially having to defend a combined Baltic states border about as long as the border of the Central Front during the Cold War (see Figure 3.1 and Table 3.1). As discussed in more detail later in the context of a wargame exercise that we conducted, this imbalance means that a Russian invasion of the Baltic states would succeed in reaching the Baltic capitals in a few days—the rapid fait accompli that NATO conventional forces were postured to prevent during the Cold War.

Enhancing NATO conventional forces in and around the Baltic states suitable to prevent a rapid Russian fait accompli is one option that NATO has explored for deterring an invasion there. Such forces, which would have to be ready to conduct combat at any time and have the permission to do so, could make it clear to the Russians that if they launched an invasion, it "would instead trigger a prolonged and serious war between Russia and a materially far wealthier and more powerful coalition, a war Moscow must fear it would be likely to lose"

**Figure 3.1**
**NATO's Cold War Central Front and 2018 Baltic Front Lines**

SOURCE: Shlapak and Johnson, 2016.

(Shlapak and Johnson, 2016, p. 2).[10] Table 3.2 displays the 2018 NATO force posture and two enhanced postures that, based on the results of RAND-conducted wargames, have the potential to prevent that rapid fait accompli. The Enhanced 1 force would slow the Russian invasion and potentially cause some or all of the Russian forces to culminate short of all the Baltic capitals. The Enhanced 2 force would achieve roughly the same NATO-to-Russian conventional force ratio as that during the Cold War along the Central Front between NATO and

[10] See Shlapak and Johnson, 2016. Given the relative proximity of the Baltic states to Moscow, Russia might see (or claim to see) enhanced NATO conventional forces as enabling an invasion by NATO. This possibility will presumably influence NATO decisions on the size and composition enhanced NATO forces.

**Table 3.1**
**Russia-to-NATO Force Ratios in and Around the Baltic States, 2018**

| | Russia | | | | | NATO | | | | |
|---|---|---|---|---|---|---|---|---|---|---|
| System | Battalions | Tanks | IFVs | APCs | Infantry Company | Battalions | Tanks | IFVs | APCs | Infantry Company |
| Maneuver brigades | | | | | | | | | | |
| Tank/ABCT | 9 | 279 | 90 | 0 | 9 | 4 | 87 | 98 | 0 | 4 |
| Mechanized/Euro | 14 | 182 | 560 | 0 | 42 | 5 | 72 | 144 | 0 | 8 |
| Motorized/SBCT | 12 | 156 | 0 | 480 | 36 | 4 | 0 | 0 | 204 | 9 |
| Airborne/Infantry battalion | 16 | 0 | 480 | 160 | 48 | **10** | **0** | **0** | **0** | **26** |
| **Total** | **51** | **617** | **1,130** | **640** | **135** | **23** | **159** | **242** | **204** | **47** |
| Force ratios (Russia:NATO) | | | | | | 2:1 | 4:1 | 5:1 | 3:1 | 3:1 |

**Table 3.1—Continued**

| | Aggregations | | |
|---|---|---|---|
| System | Russia Total | NATO Total | Ratio |
| Attack helicopter battalion | 18 | 4 | 5:1 |
| Cannon artillery battery | 90 | 22 | 4:1 |
| Rocket artillery battery | 63 | 4 | 16:1 |
| Short-range air defense artillery battery | 96 | 4 | 24:1 |
| Long-range air defense artillery battery | 52 | 3 | 17:1 |

SOURCE: Based on data from Shlapak and Johnson, 2016; Boston et al., 2018.

NOTES: Red denotes Russian forces; blue denotes U.S. forces; and green denotes non-U.S. NATO forces. ABCT = armored brigade combat team; APC = armored personnel carrier; IFV = infantry fighting vehicle; SBCT = Stryker brigade combat team.

**Table 3.2**
**Current and Notional Enhanced NATO Force Postures**

| Posture | U.S. Maneuver Brigades |
|---|---|
| Current (2018) | 1 ABCT (rotational)<br>1 SBCT (located in Germany)<br>2 IBCT(ABN)s<br>1 SPMAGTF-CR (located in Spain) |
| Enhanced 1 | 3 ABCTs (located in Poland)<br>1 SBCT (located in Germany)<br>2 IBCT(ABN)s<br>1 SPMAGTF-CR (located in Spain) |
| Enhanced 2 | 4 ABCTs (located in Poland)<br>1 SBCT (located in Germany)<br>2 IBCT(ABN)s<br>1 SPMAGTF-CR (located in Spain) |

SOURCE: Based on data from Shlapak and Johnson, 2016.

NOTE: IBCT(ABN) = infantry brigade combat team (airborne); SPMAGTF-CR = Special Purpose Marine Air-Ground Task Force – Crisis Response.

the Warsaw Pact. What this latter force could achieve has not been explored in RAND wargames, but it is clear that it would complicate Russian decisionmaking on the course that an invasion of the Baltic states would take and its outcome at least as much as the Enhanced 1 force would.

NATO has taken significant actions since the Wales Summit in 2014, including the Readiness Action Plan (Heads of State and Government of the North Atlantic Alliance, 2016), which includes a 5,000-person Very High Readiness Joint Task Force within the NATO Response Force (McNamara, 2016). The intent is that the force could deploy within 48 hours. After the 2016 Warsaw Summit, NATO began enhancing its forward presence in the Baltic states and Poland with the rotational deployment of four multinational battalion groups. The United States is also deploying a rotational ABCT variously in the Baltic states, Bulgaria, Germany, Poland, and Romania (Danby, 2018).

The two enhanced forces could entail costs ranging from about $8 billion to $14 billion to equip and about $3 billion to $5 billion annually to operate and field with personnel (for related information, see Appendix C, especially Table C.3).

## Weakness of NATO's Infrastructure for War in the Baltic States

NATO has many weaknesses, of course, but we mention the infrastructure issue here because it is sometimes unappreciated and because it would be very costly to redress related problems.

Whatever NATO's force posture, several analyses have concluded that, unlike the situation on the Central Front during the Cold War, there is currently insufficient transportation infrastructure in Europe to support a rapid flow of forces into the Baltic states. As asserted by Fiott (2016, p. 77), "without the necessary infrastructure, including transportation networks and hubs, and energy supply lines, it will be difficult for NATO to preposition or sustain military units and ensure" that response forces are "able to deploy within a few days." Shlapak and Johnson (2016, p. 8) also note, based on findings from their Baltic-area wargame, that transporting heavy armor and support vehicles via rail across Poland and then road-marching to the conflict zone is "unlikely to take less than a week to 10 days" when deploying from Grafenwoehr, Germany.

To mitigate these issues, analysts have recommended forward-basing and prepositioning of equipment in preparation for potential conflict. Some have suggested positioning U.S. forces in Poland to minimize transport distances. Others have advocated a forward presence in the Baltic states (Maisel and Keurakis, 2018) to avoid difficulties presented by the Suwalki Gap (the 60-mile border that separates Poland and Lithuania, as shown in Figure 3.2; see Bearak, 2016). This stretch of land could be denied by Russian forces positioned in Kaliningrad unless U.S. and NATO forces were committed to and capable of keeping the gap open. Forward-basing in the Baltic states, however, brings the risk of being viewed by Russia as overly aggressive. Whether forces are forward-based or not, robust transportation infrastructure is needed to enable logistics support to flow to NATO forces during combat and to transport reinforcements that could be sent from the United States to reach the battle.

The United States began addressing European defense infrastructure deficiencies in fiscal year (FY) 2015 with the European Reassur-

**Figure 3.2**
**The Suwalki Gap Land Border Between Lithuania and Poland**

ance Initiative, which was renamed the European Deterrence Initiative in 2017. Through this initiative, the United States has committed or will commit funding toward improving defense infrastructure in Europe, although investments in transportation are limited to improvements near military installations. For example, these efforts include funds for improving airfield taxiways and constructing railheads but are primarily focused on base improvements, such as construction of parking aprons, unit support facilities, and munition storage buildings. As concluded in a DoD Inspector General assessment of the initiative, there remains risk of "insufficient transport capacity to rapidly deploy U.S., allied, and partner-nation military forces to deter aggression against" Central and Eastern European countries (DoD Inspector General, 2017).

Expanding European transportation infrastructure to enable force flows would be much more costly than 2018 budget allocations in the European Deterrence Initiative. The 2018 request was $828.2 million (Office of the Under Secretary of Defense [Comptroller], 2018). As an example, consider expanding the rail line density from Grafenwoehr, Germany, to Warsaw, Poland, a distance of approximately 850 km. Assuming a cost of €3 million per kilometer of rail (AECOM, 2011), this implies a total cost on the order of €2.5 billion. In addition, if the North-South rail line density were to be increased in Poland to further enable movement—say, from Gdansk to Krakow (550 km)—this could add €1.7 billion, with both of these costs scaling with the desired number of additional lines. Beyond rail, other infrastructure improvements will also be costly. As highlighted by Fiott (2016), European Union road network improvements are estimated at €1.5 trillion through 2030, and hundreds of billions more will be required to construct additional energy supply lines across borders. Energy security is also a risk in this scenario, given that Russia supplies oil to much of Eastern Europe (Sengupta, 2017). In addition, bridge improvement projects will likely be required to support flows through Poland and into the Baltic states.

As can be seen from this discussion, the costs to improve European infrastructure to facilitate movement into the Baltic states would appear to be at least on the order of the costs of the enhanced conventional postures (see Appendix C) and the acquisition and then operations and maintenance (O&M) of a new tactical nuclear arsenal (see Appendix D). The financial burden of improving European infrastructure, particularly improvements to transportation, would not necessarily fall entirely on the United States. Deni (2017), for example, proposes cost-sharing to forward-base U.S. ABCTs in Poland, whose annual budget for infrastructure improvements is approximately $500 million.

CHAPTER FOUR

# Limited Nuclear Options for NATO Consideration

In this chapter, we discuss the features of credible limited nuclear options, NATO's current and planned nuclear capabilities, and the choice of scenarios to examine.

## Features of Credible Limited Nuclear Options

After our review of the deterrence literature (described in Chapter Two), we sought to identify nonstrategic nuclear options that NATO could employ to deter Russian aggression against the Baltic states.[1] Characterizing a given option involves the following dimensions and their possible values:

- *escalatory purpose*: respond in kind; respond with recognizable escalation
- *character*: purely demonstrative; demonstrative with some limited military effect; militarily effective
- *targets*: tactical maneuver units, command and control, airfields, and logistics; operational-level maneuver units, command and control, airfields, and logistics; theater-strategic targets, such as command and control, missiles, air bases, and logistics; strategic targets, such as command and control, space assets, and targets housing intercontinental forces

1 Various authors have identified options; see especially Payne and Foster, 2017; Durkalec, 2018.

- *delivery mechanisms*: Army, Navy, and Air Force systems; short or long range
- *magnitude of attack:* a few; hundreds
- *timing of employment:* in response to Russian first use; first use, early in conflict, just before conventional defense begins to collapse; after such collapse in an effort to stem conventional defeat.

A limited nuclear war could be limited in any or all of these dimensions.

Avoiding collateral damage would be correlated with using low-yield weapons and, much more so, with restricting the type of targets attacked. In an extreme case, a subkiloton weapon detonated in an urban environment could cause thousands of direct civilian casualties, while a high-yield weapon detonated in a sparsely populated region might produce none. As for yield, the belief that low-yield nuclear weapons could be employed for dramatic military effect while minimizing collateral damage to civilians and the environment is controversial. Some Russian writers advocate this position, but it is not clear that the position has widespread support among Russian military planners and experts on the effects of nuclear weapons (see Chapter Three). It is known only that Soviet war planners would seek to minimize collateral damage *to their own troops*.

The United States emphasizes minimizing collateral damage in all weapon employment; it is usually seen as morally important and, intuitively, as reducing the likelihood of further escalation. The latter effect is not clear and should not be assumed about the Russians, who might reason as follows: If the aim is to stoke anxieties among enemy populations about the possibility of escalation to general war, a token demonstration of nuclear use with no collateral damage would compare unfavorably to an attack that attained both dramatic military effects *and* killed civilians. In such imagined Russian reasoning, military effects would provide evidence that the military could protect neither itself nor civilians from nuclear attack and adjust the balance of forces in the attacker's favor. The civilian casualties would serve as a focus of global media attention, forcing enemy civilians to confront the possibility that continued escalation could result in their own deaths. The threshold at which such an attack would be more likely to elicit an all-out retaliation than cow the adversary might be quite high. For instance, a nuclear attack that killed one civilian or ten civilians would not seem like justification to launch a world-ending retaliatory strike, but one that killed 100 million civilians probably would. However, attacks of the scale contemplated here (tens of thousands of civilian casualties) fall into a gray area.

## Current and Planned NATO Discriminate Nuclear Capabilities

### Background

The United States dismantled most of its NSNW after the Cold War. In accordance with the Presidential Letters of Understanding, the United States and Russia made a non–legally binding agreement to eliminate broad classes of NSNW from deployment—most notably those deployed on surface ships. In 2010, the United States eliminated the last of its sea-based NSNW, the nuclear variant of the Tomahawk Land-Attack Missile (TLAM). The only remaining U.S. tactical nuclear weapons currently deployed are B61 gravity bombs deployed in the territories of NATO allies as a show of commitment. Originally developed in the 1970s, the B61 has existed in many variants.[2]

The B61 is the only nuclear weapon employed for nuclear sharing arrangements. A modest number of B61s are deployed at a limited number of well-known storage sites in several NATO states. In peacetime, the weapons remain under U.S. physical control, and in case of war, there are plans to transfer them to their host countries (with use still subject to approval by the U.S. President) (Kamp and Remkes, 2011). The current delivery vehicles are F-16s and Panavia Tornados (Kristensen and Norris, 2014).

The B61 is both a tactical and a strategic weapon (see Table 4.1). It currently exists in five versions (or *mods*) with a range of yields. In its strategic role, the B61 is one of the two nuclear weapons carried by the

---

[2] The data reported in Table 4.1 and elsewhere in this section come from public sources and may not be accurate. The details are not important to our study.

**Table 4.1**
**Versions of the B61 Nuclear Bomb**

| Modification | Role | Delivery Platform(s) |
|---|---|---|
| Mod 3 | Tactical | F-15, F-16, Panavia Tornado |
| Mod 4 | Tactical | F-15, F-16, Panavia Tornado |
| Mod 7 | Strategic | B-2 |
| Mod 10 | Tactical | F-15, F-16, Panavia Tornado |
| Mod 11 | Strategic earth-penetrator | B-2 |
| Mod 12 | Tactical and strategic (Glide tail kit) | Expected in 2019 |

SOURCE: Kristensen and Norris, 2014, pp. 79–84.
NOTE: The data reported here are not authoritative.

B-2 bomber. Mods 3, 4, and 10 are tactical, and Mod 7 is the strategic version carried by the B-2 bomber. Mod 11 is an earth-penetrating weapon introduced in 1997 and carried by the B-2. The B61 was formerly carried by the B-52 Stratofortress, but that aircraft has apparently not been tasked with delivering nuclear gravity bombs since 2010 (Kristensen, 2017). Past and current variants lack standoff capability, but the forthcoming Mod 12 (expected in 2019) has a tail kit to enhance performance. The new version will have improved accuracy.[3] The B61 offers a variable-yield (or "dial-a-yield") capability.

The limited number of nonstrategic aircraft capable of carrying the B61 limits U.S. options for employing the B-52 in a conflict with a peer adversary, such as Russia. At present, the only U.S. aircraft rated to carry the B61 are the F-15 and F-16 fighters and the B-2. Modern Russian air defense systems pose very serious survivability challenges to the fighter aircraft, which might be destroyed well before they could drop gravity bombs on their targets.

More options are possible with strategic platforms. There are negative considerations, however. Because the B-2 stealth bomber is a strategic delivery system, using it for a limited strike might send an unin-

[3] See National Nuclear Security Administration, undated.

tended message that a full-scale U.S. strike is underway. The United States plans to deploy a nuclear-capable version of the stealthy F-35 Joint Strike Fighter to provide an alternative means of delivering the B61 Mod 12 to targets protected by modern air defense systems. This will probably not be available until 2025 or so, and, as discussed later, the ability of the F-35 to penetrate the Russian IADS and deliver a B61 is not assured. In addition, the NATO bases hosting dual-capable aircraft are vulnerable to attack by Russian NSNW.

Open reports suggest that the B61s in Europe serve primarily as evidence of U.S. alliance commitments. NATO does not plan specific nuclear use against any country but maintains an adaptive planning capability. That is sometimes interpreted as a lack of seriousness, as in an open study that claimed that there were no programmed targets for the bombs, although the same study acknowledged that NATO forces regularly conducted drills about their delivery (Kristensen, 2012). The evolution of the post-1991 security environment has eroded even further the ability of non-U.S. NATO allies to employ B61s against Russia. During the Cold War, it was envisioned that the United States would release these weapons to its NATO allies after the start of hostilities and that these allied militaries would (with U.S. authorization) employ the bombs against enemy targets either on friendly or Warsaw Pact territory. The Cold War strategic standoff offered a rich set of possible targets for limited nuclear attack, including high-value fixed Soviet military facilities in East Germany that were in easy range for such aircraft as the F-15, F-16, and Panavia Tornado. In a NATO-Russia conflict in the Baltic states, however, the nearest Russian military targets would be in Kaliningrad, Russia. Such older aircraft probably also have very limited survivability in the face of a modern Russian IADS. The introduction of nuclear-capable F-35s in the next decade will improve this situation, but the bases hosting B61s and nuclear-capable aircraft may themselves be targets of a Russian nuclear (or conventional) strike.

An additional nuclear delivery option providing a somewhat flexible low-yield capability is the AGM-86 ALCM carried by B-52H bombers. This weapon originally entered service in 1982 and carries a variable-yield W80 nuclear warhead. It has a range of more than 2,400 km. The nuclear-armed variant of the AGM-86 employs a relatively inaccurate inertial guidance system, limiting its utility for low-yield precision applications. Also, the survivability and effectiveness of this aged system is in doubt. Even in the 1980s, concerns that Soviet air defenses could defeat the AGM-86 led to the deployment of its stealthier, more accurate, longer-range successor, the AGM-129 ALCM. The AGM-129 was in service from 1990 until 2012 but was retired due to O&M challenges.

**Initiatives of the Nuclear Posture Review**

According to the 2018 Nuclear Posture Review, the United States needs to develop and field new low-yield nuclear options to deter possible Russian use of its NSNW. The document specifically calls for two options: a low-yield warhead for the Trident D2 SLBM as an immediate-term measure and a new nuclear-armed SLCM for the intermediate term.

The Nuclear Posture Review stipulates that

> DoD and National Nuclear Security Administration (NNSA) will develop for deployment a low-yield SLBM warhead to ensure a prompt response option that is able to penetrate adversary defenses. This is a comparatively low-cost and near term modification . . . that will help counter any mistaken perception of an exploitable "gap" in U.S. regional deterrence capabilities. (DoD, 2018, p. xii)

Despite its low yield, as the Nuclear Posture Review points out, the W76-2 will technically be a strategic system and will be accountable under New START limits.

The prospect of a low-yield Trident warhead has elicited considerable controversy, resulting partly from fears that the Russians might be able to use the launch to localize a nuclear-powered ballistic missile submarine and target it in retaliation. These concerns may be overblown and were apparently discounted in testimony by the commander of U.S. Strategic Command (Hyten, 2018). However, a more concerning possibility is that Russia might determine its symmetrical response to be targeting not the ballistic missile submarine but an equivalent U.S. target, potentially within the continental United States, using a similar-yield warhead. Such a strike might employ a low-yield SLBM warhead (e.g., a possible low-yield variant of the Russian Bulava SLBM) or low-yield warheads from intercontinental ballistic missiles or ALCMs.

The 2018 Nuclear Posture Review states, "for the longer term the United States will pursue a nuclear-armed SLCM, leveraging existing technologies to help ensure its cost effectiveness" (DoD, 2018, p. xii). The document does not specify whether the new nuclear SLCM will be a variant of the venerable Tomahawk missile or a nuclear variant of the future Next-Generation Land-Attack Weapon, although the document's language suggests the former. Because the nuclear variant of the TLAM was decommissioned in the early 2010s and its W80 warheads were dismantled, it is not possible to simply return these weapons to service. A modern nuclear-armed Tomahawk could exploit guidance-system advancements of its conventional versions, enabling more-discriminating nuclear employment options. It will almost certainly employ a variant of the W80 family of warheads (including the W84 and W85), which include a variable-yield capability. The Nuclear Posture Review states that the

> SLCM will provide a needed non-strategic regional presence, an assured response capability. It also will provide an arms control compliant response to Russia's non-compliance with the Intermediate-range Nuclear Forces Treaty, its non-strategic nuclear arsenal, and its other destabilizing behaviors. (DoD, 2018, p. xii)

Other new U.S. nuclear delivery systems may enable discriminate nuclear employment. For example, the Long-Range Stand-Off weapon is intended to replace the AGM-86 ALCM. The intention for this missile is to maintain viability of the nuclear-armed manned bomber against highly sophisticated future air defenses. This system is in relatively early development but will probably be analogous to its Russian counterparts, the Kh-101 and Kh-102. It will probably have a variable-yield warhead, a range of several thousand kilometers, and an ability to penetrate the Russian anti-access, area denial bubble in Eastern Europe. It will be deployed on the B-52H, the B-21, and possibly the B-2 bombers (i.e., from strategic delivery systems).

In addition to the W76-2, the SLCM, and the Long-Range Stand-Off weapon, all currently in active development, various other NSNW have been proposed (Kroenig, 2016). These include nuclear variants of the Joint Air-to-Surface Standoff Missile (an ALCM) and the DeepStrike short-range ballistic missile (which is analogous to Russia's Iskander-M). Developing and certifying nuclear capability for these systems might be relatively expensive because they were not originally designed for a nuclear role. Others have suggested developing a U.S. counterpart of the SSC-8 or a Pershing III missile that might be analogous to Russia's mothballed RS-26 Rubezh. Some of these proposals seek to gain bargaining leverage to convince the Russians to negotiate limits on NSNW or reduce the appearance of an NSNW capability gap with the Russians. A potential drawback of developing and deploying these systems is that doing so could precipitate a total collapse of the Intermediate-Range Nuclear Forces Treaty, which Moscow could blame on the United States, opening the door for Russia to be even more aggressive in its development of theater-range nuclear-capable delivery systems.

All of these proposed nuclear delivery systems have inadequacies for extended deterrence in Eastern Europe. None is obviously suitable for nuclear sharing arrangements like those employed with the B61. Most importantly, these systems will not, in and of themselves, provide NATO with discriminate or employable nuclear options. Accurate, low-yield weapons are necessary but insufficient. The 2018 Nuclear Posture Review specifically states that developing low-yield options such as the W76-2 and SLCM "is not intended to enable, nor does it enable, 'nuclear war-fighting'" (DoD, 2018, p. xii). This assessment is correct, but—for the same reason—these systems will not obviously enhance deterrence. To be credible and proportional, employment options require appropriate *targets*, as well as the weapons with which to attack them. This gives the adversary a vote in the matter, and in the case of an invasion of the Baltic states, it is difficult to identify good targets for NATO to attack that would significantly affect Russian military operations.

## Scenario Development Considerations

The number of possible scenarios in which NATO might use a nuclear weapon was far too large to examine in a limited study. Thus, we considered a smaller set of scenarios, all of which were either designed into the wargame exercise described in Chapter Six or included in "what if" discussions during and after the game. The scenarios that we examined were as follows:

1. Demonstrative use (one to three weapons) in the battle area strictly external to Russia intended to demonstrate willingness and ability to use nuclear weapons but with minimum casualties and no significant military effect.
   - Variant: Use on isolated, significant, but noncritical military targets (e.g., one airfield, one maneuver unit).
2. Demonstrative use deeper into theater, perhaps into Russia itself.
3. Restrained, small-scale use for military effect in the operational theater of war. This might involve tens of weapons against a mix of ground forces, missiles, airfields, and so forth constrained by magnitude, necessity (use where most needed, not elsewhere), and avoidance of strategic targets (e.g., Russia's intercontinental nuclear forces, command and control, and perhaps space assets).
4. Employment for tactical effectiveness in blunting or defeating an attack. This might involve tens or hundreds of weapons.
   - Variant: Demonstrative strikes against targets in Russia.

Outcomes similar to those of the four scenarios could be achieved with strikes using strategic systems (e.g., a Trident or stealthy cruise missile with low-yield weapons) undertaken in a way that makes it as clear as possible to Russia that NATO's nuclear use was limited. This option would exist even if NATO had no tactical or theater-nuclear weapons.

Many observers rule out such options, fearing that Russian leadership would misinterpret use of strategic platforms as a strategic attack requiring full-scale response. Others disagree; for example, a national academy panel disagreed after long debate related to options for prompt global strike (National Research Council, 2008). If options using strategic platforms had been part of U.S. doctrine for some time and had been exercised and even advertised, Russian intelligence would not likely be confused. Even with the shortcomings of current Russian warning systems, is it plausible that a limited nuclear use in the context in question would be misinterpreted? Gen John Hyten, commander of U.S. Strategic Command, has been sanguine on the matter based on how he believes he would react (with caution and restraint) in an analogous launch from Russia (Hyten, 2018). In our view, the biggest risk—but one common to all limited nuclear options—is that, even though the immediate attack might be limited, the adversary would see general nuclear war as inevitable and full-scale preemption as necessary. Another concern is that a Trident missile launched for a limited strike in a Baltic-area conflict—for example, targeting airfields in western Russia—might, for some minutes after launch, be indistinguishable from a missile launched at Moscow. Thus, the possibility that it would trigger a massive Russian response cannot be precluded, especially if a launch-under-attack option were activated. During the Cold War, the Soviets were extremely concerned about the possibility that NATO's Pershing missile would be used for a quick and sudden (6–8 minute) strike on Moscow (Getler, 1982).

CHAPTER FIVE

# Selected Methods for Evaluating Deterrence Options

Thus far, we have presented basic concepts of deterrence for use in examining possible nuclear options for NATO in deterring Russia. Another issue is how to assess such options. Historically, analyses have been based largely on written or oral qualitative arguments. It is possible, however, to bring to bear some more-analytic methods that can sharpen issues and reveal insights. Two such methods are (1) human wargaming and computerized game-structured modeling and (2) relatively simple and qualitative cognitive modeling. We do not discuss exchange calculations of the sort popular with analysts during parts of the Cold War because these calculations would not be obviously relevant and were quite misleading even during the Cold War (Davis, 1989).

## Wargaming and Game-Structured Modeling

When issues are not well understood, human wargaming can sometimes be very instructive. Wargames may quickly yield an understanding of geography, military realities, nominal perspectives, and the military and political actions that a nation's leaders might take—that is, the *possible moves*. The games might help establish the *game board* and the *game rules*. As emphasized by Schelling decades ago, one of the primary values of wargaming can be to educate and socialize senior officials. They can come up to speed quickly and gain shared knowledge to draw upon in later contexts. The wargames can break down mental barriers, open minds, and reveal new options (see Levine, Schelling, and Jones, 1991, Chapter Two). To be sure, however, such games have shortcomings, and the insights from games may be less informative than insights obtained in other ways (e.g., personal experiences; analogies to historical incidents; or outputs of mathematical models, which can be overfocused on easily measurable considerations, such as force ratios). As Schelling noted, insights are so important that we should be happy to have new mechanisms for obtaining them. As always, however, subsequent work is necessary to see if the insights hold up to scrutiny (Schelling, 1987).

DoD has been reinvigorating the use of human-run gaming in recent years—a trend instigated by former Deputy Secretary of Defense Robert Work. These efforts continue.

In principle, it is possible to use game-structured simulation in which human teams or artificial-intelligence models can be used interchangeably. Doing so permits great improvements in the ability to reproduce experiments, vary assumptions systematically, and explore a large scenario space. Such efforts, however, can be very expensive and both technically and intellectually challenging. They are rare.[1] Human wargaming, sometimes with some computer assistance, is more common.

## Qualitative and Semiquantitative Cognitive Modeling

When real-world decisionmakers contemplate the potential for escalation in war, it is possible to capture a great many of the issues with relatively simple cognitive models that attempt to represent an opponent's reasoning during a potential crisis (and, indeed, the reasoning of one's allies and even one's own government). Qualitative models can specify the factors in judgments and decisions, possible logic for decisionmakers combining those factors to reach conclusions, and the options avail-

[1] For a brief discussion of the RAND Strategy Assessment System in the 1980s, see National Research Council, 2014.

able. The purpose of such models can be to collect and organize all of the known considerations, which might otherwise exist only in the minds of officials, analysts, and wargamers, or—to some extent—in scholarly journals and books.

In the approach that RAND researchers have used over the years (Davis, 2002), a primary purpose of such modeling is to identify *alternative* ways in which protagonists may be reasoning. Doing so breaks away from the "tyranny of the best estimate" (Davis, 2002, p. 242). If history demonstrates anything convincingly, it is that nations' best estimates of opponent reasoning have often been seriously wrong. Furthermore, the uncritical embrace of best estimates has ill effects on military and diplomatic strategies. Strategies should be flexible (allowing for different missions and objectives), adaptive to circumstances, and robust to adverse shocks. Achieving that flexibility is easier when diverse possibilities have been anticipated.

The earliest example of qualitative cognitive modeling was an assessment of Saddam Hussein. In 1990, standard intelligence assessments of Saddam Hussein described a war-weary, risk-averse, and sometimes culture-sensitive figure who would not be aggressive while licking wounds from the previous war with Iran. RAND researchers constructed alternative cognitive models of Saddam to dramatize the different possible interpretations of existing evidence. One model adhered closely to the best-estimate image, but another model (also based on extensive information, such as Saddam's speeches and writings) described him as angry; victimized by his neighbors, the United States, and the United Kingdom; entitled; and grandiose. In this latter model, Saddam was willing to take what the United States would see as risks; was contemptuous of the United States and U.S. allies; and would take actions necessary for himself, as a great man of history, to correct the mistreatment of Iraq.

Initially, the models were treated as parallel, with either being plausible. As events developed in the real 1990 crisis, having the second model as a possibility allowed U.S. leaders to recognize early that the more aggressive Saddam model was more accurate and that Saddam was indeed going to invade Iraq. A RAND seminar game on the matter influenced a senior intelligence officer (Patrick Lang), who soon became the first to predict that the invasion would occur (Woodward, 1991). After Saddam's invasion but before the counteroffensive, use of that model also suggested that—contrary to common fears among U.S. planners—Saddam would probably *not* pull out of Kuwait preemptively, although he would quit if war began and he found himself losing. These insights were discussed with senior national-security officials in 1990 and 1991. Basics of the Saddam model appear to have been solid, based on what is now known about Saddam's thinking between 1989 and 1991.

Similar modeling in the 1990s, albeit with less information, concluded that Kim Jong Il would not give up his nuclear program. He might promise to do so, but the factors favoring continuation were too compelling—for each of a variety of modeled mindsets of Kim Jong Il. RAND researchers suggested to DoD leaders that the United State should seek objectives other than complete elimination of North Korean nuclear weapons, such as limits on testing and missiles and less-threatening conventional postures (Arquilla and Davis, 1994).

Cognitive models can help us avoid mirror imaging and understand how other heads of state might be reasoning. The same issues are under discussion in 2018 with respect to Kim Jong Un. A new book by former Director of National Intelligence James R. Clapper reinforces our view that North Korea has deep fears of a U.S. invasion and will not truly and fully denuclearize, unless conceivably at the end of a many-year process with many elements (Clapper, 2018). Nonetheless, many options are possible.

## Using Human Wargames to Test and Supplement Cognitive Models

### Methods Applied to a Korea Scenario

In 2015 and 2016, RAND collaborated with South Korea's Korea Institute for Defense Analyses in using cognitive modeling to prepare for and guide human wargaming. The idea was to think through issues that might arise in a much more serious crisis than had yet occurred—one in which war, even nuclear war, was plausible. Earlier work had indicated that extended deterrence was in serious trouble and that crisis with nuclear options on the table was likely or even inevitable (Davis et al., 2016). The project team also anticipated that, when such a crisis arose, it would be necessary to seriously contemplate the unthinkable—for example, preventive-war attack on North Korea. The U.S. President would insist on doing so. At the time, addressing such a possibility was, to South Koreans, to address the unthinkable. Doing so, however, proved prescient. One benefit was a more fulsome understanding of why such preventive-war attack would probably be ineffective and risky.

Figure 5.1 displays the overview construct of the effort in 2015 and 2016, some of which is described in a publicly available working paper (Davis, 2017).

The model developed for the project pulled together existing strategic theory. It generated rough quantitative measures of war outcomes intended only to reveal issues and magnitudes. Preliminary work using the model allowed the RAND and Korea Institute for Defense Analyses team to design a human wargame that would raise especially important issues and prod participants on sensitive matters. When the actual

**Figure 5.1**
**A Merged Construct for Using Both Human Wargames and Cognitive Modeling**

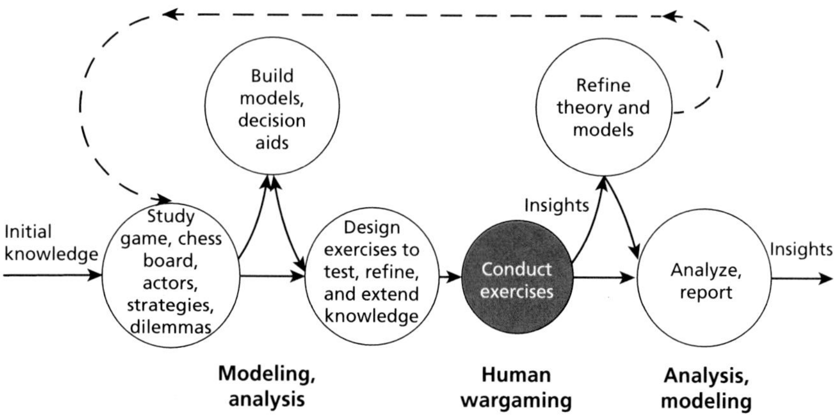


SOURCE: Davis, 2017.

wargame was conducted, the teams largely behaved remarkably as anticipated by the model. However, the human wargame's role-playing teams for North Korea and China, as well as for South Korea, raised some additional considerations and options. One example that stood out was that the China team assessed the situation and its options very differently (and more cautiously) than expected. Such insights could then be rolled over into a revised version of the model (from unpublished RAND research), which was mature enough to suggest decision aids for use in further human wargames.

### Modeling Russia

Whether correctly or not, it is usually assumed that President Putin and the Russian government are rational actors, albeit actors with misperceptions and cognitive biases. That is, they are subject to the usual shortcomings of limited rationality. It is likely, although by no means certain, that Russian leadership in a future crisis would be similar in this respect. Although elements of the Russian military may believe that meaningful victory is possible in nuclear war, especially in limited nuclear war, we do not know whether President Putin buys into that mindset, and we have reasons to doubt it (Oliker and Baklitskiy, 2018). He may see nuclear weapons, brandishing of such weapons, and even conceivable use of such weapons as part of a competition of mind games. And, if nuclear weapons were used, he could be very interested in bringing about war termination. Whatever his views, in a battle of wills—what many analysts would see as a game of chicken—Putin might not be very impressed by NATO using nuclear weapons in a way that was essentially symbolic rather than militarily effective, especially if NATO lacked credible ways to ratchet up the level of nuclear use incrementally. Based on Russian behavior, and Soviet behavior before that, we see it as likely that Russia would use opportunities for a fait accompli but would be wary of risks otherwise. After all, it is Russia that has come a long way in perfecting gray-zone warfare.

## Recommendation on Methods

For the purposes of this study on how to use nuclear forces to improve deterrence against a Russian invasion of the Baltic states, we saw value in a combination of methods:

- Human wargaming using, for example, commercial board games adapted for purpose, or special-purpose wargames developed from scratch, to better understand military geography, military options, and the rough usefulness of battlefield nuclear weapons and possible limited nuclear options.
- Rough, brainstorming-level cognitive modeling and related seminar gaming to better identify factors and logics of a more qualitative nature. We anticipate that such work would sharpen understanding of risk calculations and identify different considerations for contemplating nonstrategic nuclear options.
- Next-step cognitive modeling to represent the previous two methods in qualitative computerized models to allow exploration across the scenario space.
- Next-step human gaming to test and enrich the modeling. Multiple games would be necessary, but the games conducted should be designed specifically to reflect solid knowledge from the preexisting model and to exploit human play to test or supplement aspects that are not well understood.

For the study detailed in this report, we used a combination of the first two approaches. The third and fourth methods were not feasible to pursue within the project's limited resources.

CHAPTER SIX

# Wargaming the Use of Nonstrategic Nuclear Weapons During an Invasion of the Baltic States

To explore what could occur if NSNW were employed by either NATO or Russia during a conflict involving the Baltic states, we conducted a wargame exercise using the RAND Framework for Live Exercises (R-FLEX).[1] The game included a great deal of discussion about "what ifs" rather than following a single course. Most of these scenarios had been anticipated by prior thinking, using a lesser version of the methods discussed in Chapter Five. As discussed in the remainder of this chapter, the most significant insight from the game—and one that we regard as robust—is that NATO lacks escalation dominance. Indeed, Russia enjoys escalation dominance. Once nuclear weapons were used in the game, NATO suffered more from continued nuclear attacks on its targets in Europe than Russia suffered from nuclear attacks on its maneuver forces, airfields, assembly and support areas, and other targets in Russia. At any point after NSNW were employed, NATO had a stronger military incentive to de-escalate than Russia did. We recognized that it was possible that higher-level considerations would come into play and that Russian leaders would be so worried about general nuclear war as to seek peace. Participants, however, felt that the credibility of such a NATO (or U.S.) escalation from local war in the Baltic

[1] For a description of R-FLEX, see RAND Corporation, 2016, and Appendix B to this report. The particular gaming exercise described in this chapter included nine RAND analysts, most with extensive experience in gaming, whether as military officers before joining RAND, as civilians in DoD, or in earlier RAND wargaming studies. The game drew heavily on other RAND R-FLEX gaming, as described in Appendix B.

states to general nuclear war was much lower than that of NATO's limited nuclear options during the Cold War.

In the following sections, we describe the wargame exercise, beginning with the initiating scenario (expressed in present tense, as it was presented to participants) and then developments from the exercise.

## The Initiating Scenario

In the 2020s, a crisis has been unfolding for seven to eight weeks, with Russia preparing forces in its Western Military District to invade the Baltic states. This relatively short-notice invasion is very demanding for NATO, given current posture, readiness, and capabilities (Shlapak and Johnson, 2016).

The Russian land forces available on short notice in the Western Military District include elements from the 6th Combined Arms Army, the 1st Guards Tank Army, and the 20th Guards Combined Arms Army. These include multiple tank, motorized rifle, and airborne brigades and divisions; artillery, multiple rocket launcher, and tactical missile brigades; air defense formations providing layered coverage from the Ground Forces and Aerospace Forces; and attack aviation brigades and regiments.

The NATO forces include four Enhanced Forward Presence multinational battlegroups of, at most, battalion size. These groups are led by the United Kingdom, Canada, Germany, and the United States; they are deployed throughout Estonia, Latvia, Lithuania, and Poland on a rotational basis. A mechanized infantry brigade is mobilizing in Poland. Other NATO and U.S. forces in theater include an SBCT, an ABCT, and an infantry brigade (see Figure 6.1).

Russia has dispersed its combat and logistics forces to limit the damage that any particular NSNW used against them can cause, as well as to limit the effectiveness of NATO precision weapons, such as the Small Diameter Bomb. Russian tactical dispersion is similar to that developed in response to potential NATO nuclear use during the Cold War: Battalion-sized combat groups will be moving along multiple lines of advance with sufficient spacing to ensure that no two groups will be within the footprint of a single weapon.

**Figure 6.1**
**NATO and Russian Forces in and Around the Baltic States**

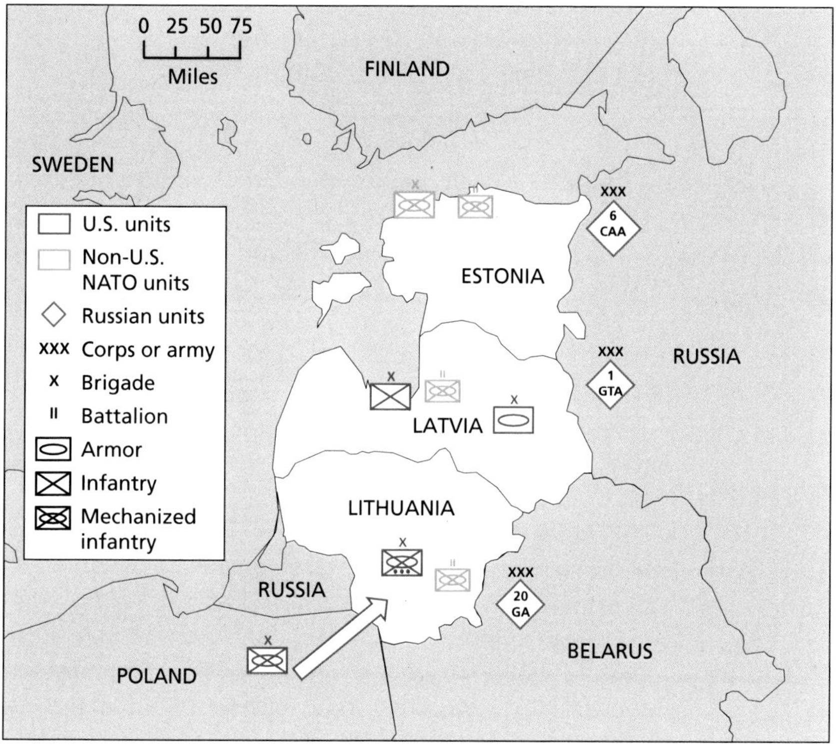


SOURCE: Adapted from information in Shlapak and Johnson, 2016.

As shown in wargames that RAND has conducted during the past several years, and incorporating variations of the conventional forces postulated for this game, Russian forces can reach the outskirts of one or more Baltic capitals in less than three days (Shlapak and Johnson, 2016). This quick and relatively easy conventional victory occurs because Russia can do the following (Bonds and Tarraf, 2017):

- Disrupt NATO command, control, and communications with cyberattacks and electronic warfare.
- Deny NATO quick air superiority using Russia's numerous mobile and capable short- and long-range IADSs.

- Jam the Global Positioning System, thereby disrupting NATO targeting and attacks using precision munitions.
- Defeat NATO artillery using standoff artillery and rocket fires.
- Overrun or bypass Baltic state border defenses.
- Destroy NATO infantry using massed fires.
- Move rapidly along multiple lines of attack.

Thus, NATO forces can be rapidly isolated and overwhelmed if they do not rapidly fall back to the Baltic capitals. If NATO forces do fall back, they will be isolated in the capitals and cut off from resupply and sustainment. Whatever NATO does, Shlapak and Johnson observe,

> Such a rapid defeat would leave NATO with a limited number of options, all bad: a bloody counteroffensive at some point, fraught with escalatory risk, to liberate the Baltic states; to escalate itself, as it threatened to do to avert defeat during the Cold War; or to concede at least temporary defeat, with uncertain but predictably disastrous consequences for the Alliance and, not incidentally, the people of the Baltic states. (Shlapak and Johnson, 2016, p. 1)

Our wargame exercise explored cases in which NATO escalates and uses NSNW either (1) *first (and early)* in an attempt to damage and destroy Russia's forces and blunt the Russian conventional attack or shock the Russians into halting their invasion or (2) for analogous reasons, *after* Russia uses nuclear weapons to attack NATO targets.

As discussed previously, NATO's NSNW stockpile currently comprises a modest number of B61 air-delivered bombs at a limited number of well-known air bases in NATO member states. The B61 is a gravity bomb; a variant with a tail kit will have improved accuracy. B61s must be delivered from relatively close range. Thus, when used early in conflict against Russian forces protected by capable Russian IADSs, successful penetration is not assured even by stealth aircraft, such as the B-2 or F-35 Joint Strike Fighter (see Figure 6.2). Furthermore, the availability of B61s is not assured because they are stored in a small number of well-known locations that can be attacked, pre-

**Figure 6.2**
**Russian Integrated Air Defense Systems Around the Baltic States**

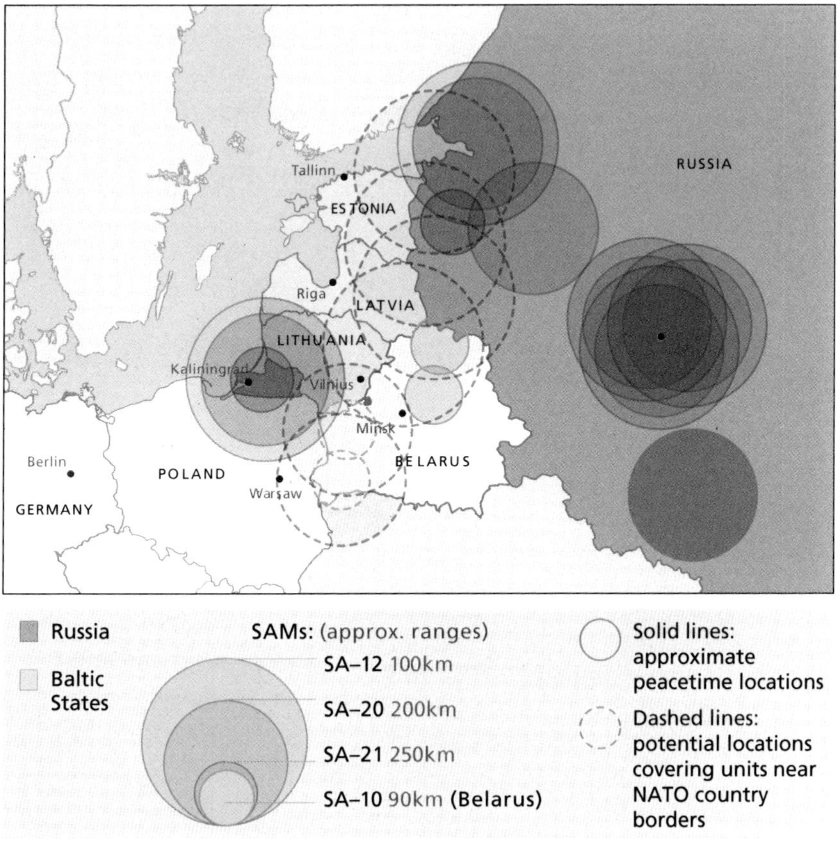


SOURCE: Boston et al., 2018, p. 10.
NOTES: Orange circles show Belarusian air defenses, which are integrated into the Russian network. SAM = surface-to-air missile.

emptively or otherwise.[2] Other (postulated) NSNW are available that could penetrate the IADS early and throughout the conflict. These weapons include ballistic missiles and stealth cruise missiles launched

---

[2] During the Cold War, NATO based NSNW at many locations in West Germany alone (Arkin and Fieldhouse, 1985). It had more than 5,000 nonstrategic nuclear warheads (Norris and Kristensen, 2011).

from ships or submarines; standoff air-delivered missiles; and nuclear-armed versions of Army systems, such as the Army Tactical Missile System. Basing, command and control, and targeting considerations are assumed (not discussed in any detail here).[3] Weapons with a 50-kiloton yield that can reach their intended targets, along with targeting information and permissions for use, are assumed to be available.

In contrast to NATO's stockpile, as discussed previously, Russia has a more diverse set of about 2,000 NSNW deliverable by air and naval platforms, and with greater assurance of surviving and hitting targets, for its use in such a conflict (Majumdar, 2017).

## How the Wargame Exercise Unfolded

The game was not a path through a single scenario but rather a series of discussions that considered many "what if" scenarios. In the sections that follow, however, we organize the discussion to cover the instances in which NATO is first to use a nuclear weapon and then the instances in which Russia is.

### NATO Uses Nuclear Weapons First

First nuclear use by NATO is very seldom contemplated today but was a key element of NATO's concept of deterrence during the Cold War. Under a flexible response approach, NATO was prepared to use a conventional defense if attacked by a Warsaw Pact member. However, if that defense was failing, NATO was prepared to escalate to using nuclear weapons, perhaps by first launching a small or limited demonstration attack against military targets to convince the Warsaw Pact that it should halt its invasion. That is, NATO was prepared to use nuclear weapons first, if necessary, to re-establish deterrence. Although it has obviously de-emphasized the use of nuclear weapons, NATO still allows for it: "Nuclear weapons are a core component of the Alliance's overall capabilities for deterrence and defence alongside conventional and missile defence forces" (NATO, 2018a).

---

[3] An SLBM would have to be capable of being retargeted in flight to hit moving or mobile targets.

### *Attack Russian Maneuver Units en Masse?*

In our wargame exercise, NATO commanders knew that they would be rapidly overwhelmed by the Russian forces and considered early first use of NSNW to prevent that outcome; but, the commanders wondered, what would NATO target? Destroying a substantial number of the Russian maneuver units would require using a few hundred nuclear weapons: Russian forces (more than 60 battalions) were highly dispersed because there was little reason for them to concentrate barring a significant opposing NATO ground force.[4] NATO would need three to five moderate-yield nuclear weapons to effectively destroy each battalion.[5] The battalions could be targeted early in their assembly areas inside Russia or later inside the Baltic countries; in the latter case, even more weapons per battalion would be needed depending on targeting information about moving maneuver forces. The Russian forces would advance rapidly through populated areas toward the Baltic capitals, which would likely cause civilians of the Baltic states to flee ahead of and around the advancing forces. Thus, unless nuclear attacks were conducted against the Russian forces very early during their advance, substantial civilian deaths and casualties would occur, as well as substantial damage to civilian infrastructure. The wargame exercise participants considered it unlikely that NATO would decide to employ large numbers of nuclear weapons early in the conflict in an attempt to destroy a substantial amount of the Russian forces—either in their

---

4 Across the Western Military District, the Russian force included 23 brigades or regiments, each with up to three maneuver battalion tactical groups from the Ground Forces and Airborne Forces. This reflected the Russian force structure as currently anticipated for 2019 and 2020, augmented to full strength or reinforced by elements of the other nine combined arms armies in the Russian ground order of battle.

5 For game purposes, we considered the attacking formations as a mix of armored and unarmored forces that typically make up a Russian battalion tactical group. Kill mechanisms would be a mix of prompt radiation, dynamic pressure, and overpressure. The forces in armored vehicles would primarily be affected by radiation because the vehicles are resistant to blast, while the light vehicles and personnel would be affected by blast and overpressure, as well as radiation. The selection of weapon yield would be dependent on the formation area, concern over collateral damage, and the number of weapons that might be allowed to be used (one of the game moves considered was the number of weapons allowed to be fired, because the opponent could possibly gauge the strength of its response based on the number of weapons fired, rather than yield and target selected).

assembly areas in Russia proper, which would offer the possibility of dramatic escalation by Russia, or in the Baltic states, where such use might not be supported by those countries' citizens and governments. Later (certainly after the first 12 hours) use of large numbers of weapons after the Russian forces had advanced would amount to destroying the Baltic states in order to save them. Thus, the participants gave no further consideration to employing nuclear weapons to destroy a substantial number of the invading Russian forces.

### *Attack Selected Military Targets?*

As the game proceeded, participants considered conducting first and early nuclear attacks using a few weapons to inflict real but limited damage against such military targets as a Russian long-range (SA-20 or SA-21) air defense system and a single maneuver battalion that had crossed the border into the Baltic states. Roughly three to six weapons would be needed to do so. The participants also considered attacks on air defenses in Kaliningrad (the Russian enclave between Poland and the Baltic states), as well as attacks on the Russian Baltic fleet in Kaliningrad. The latter attacks, while requiring limited numbers of weapons, would likely cause substantial numbers of Russian civilian deaths and casualties, potentially prompting a substantial escalation, and were ruled out for that reason. Attacks on air bases in western Russia were considered but were also ruled out. Militarily, those bases house aircraft that are overmatched by NATO aircraft. They are not essential to the success of Russia's invading forces (Figure 6.3). Attacking the bases in Russia proper would also be risky, raising the distinct possibility of a strong escalatory response. So, the wargame exercise proceeded with a NATO attack using five nuclear weapons to destroy a Russian mobile long-range air defense system that had been fortuitously located and a single Russian maneuver battalion, both inside the Latvian border.[6]

---

[6] RAND wargames generally indicate that it is difficult for NATO and the United States to find battlefield targets as the Russians rapidly advance. NATO airborne reconnaissance systems must stand off because of Russian air defenses, and use of space-based assets can be complex in the environment that the Russians can create. Russian electronic warfare capabilities further complicate NATO operations. NATO knows where the Russian forces are headed but has difficulty performing precise targeting. To be sure, later in a more extended

**Figure 6.3**
**Potential Airfield Targets in Western Russia**

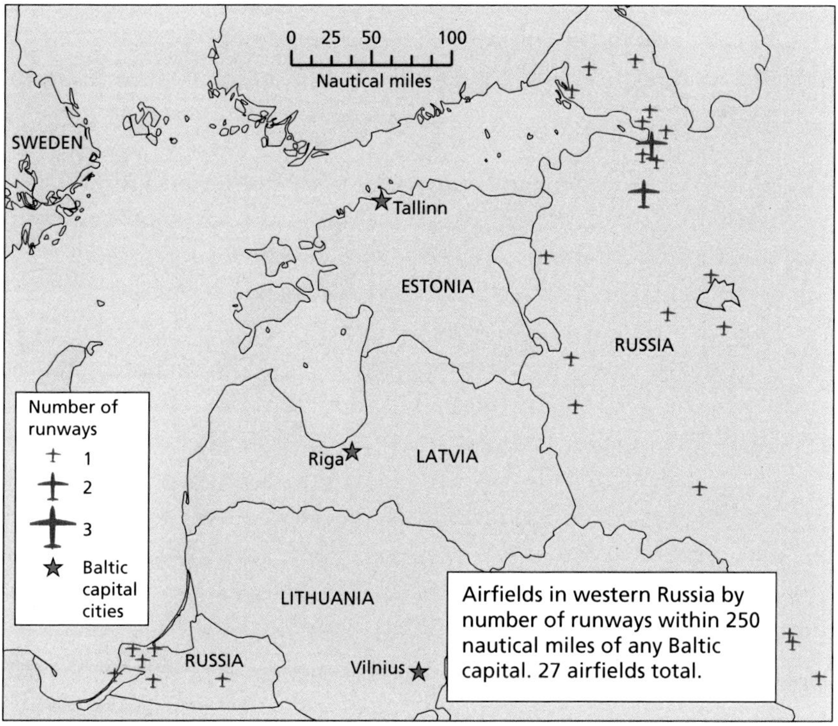


SOURCE: Authors' analysis based on releasable information in National Geospatial-Intelligence Agency, 2010.
NOTE: Only runways longer than 5,000 ft are included.

### *Russian Response*

Next, the participants considered how the Russians might react. Options included the following:

- Be shocked by NATO's first and early use of nuclear weapons, decide that they had miscalculated in their expectation of a quick and relatively easy victory, and halt their invasion.

---

conflict, Russian air defenses might well be seriously degraded, which is one of the concerns that Russian military planners think about. This may well be one of the reasons for Russian interest in a first-nuclear-use option.

- Continue advancing their forces without responding with the use of nuclear weapons.
- Escalate strongly and attack a large number of targets throughout Europe and possibly in the United States.
- Respond in kind and employ a limited number of nuclear weapons against NATO targets.

Wargame exercise participants discussed these options as follows.

*Russia is shocked into halting the invasion.* The participants considered this reaction to be possible but with unknown likelihood. Cold War work using the RAND Strategy Assessment System found a case in which the Soviets halted a hypothetical Warsaw Pact invasion of western Europe when NATO employed NSNW immediately, on the first day of the war (Davis, 1989). The model's logic was that the Soviets halted the invasion because, in effect, they decided that they had completely miscalculated; that the sides were on the threshold of general nuclear war; and, importantly, that the die was not completely cast and their prospects if war continued were exceedingly uncertain. In contrast, the same models predicted that the Soviets would continue fighting if NATO used nuclear weapons later in the conflict, after it was clear that a Soviet victory was close. For our Baltic-area wargame exercise, participants considered there to be a low probability that NATO would be willing to engage in general thermonuclear war to preserve the independence of the Baltic states.[7] Furthermore, game participants seriously doubted that Russian leaders would regard the threat of such escalation to be credible.[8] Thus, participants were skepti-

---

[7] Game participants were uncomfortable making sweeping statements about what NATO might do, because such statements might seem to undercut basic elements of long-standing NATO strategy. However, the commitment of NATO nations to defend any member who is attacked is not a commitment for all members to be willing to take steps that put themselves in mortal danger. Rather, NATO should reasonably accomplish its deterrent objectives in ways that are more credible than depending on the specter of unleashing general nuclear war over a dispute in the Baltic states. We discuss those more-credible ways later in the report.

[8] Russia may have noticed that, as a candidate, President Trump made statements indicating less than a firm commitment to defending the Baltic states—or, for that matter, NATO writ large (see Taylor and Birnbaum, 2016).

cal that the Russians would halt and, therefore, went on to consider the other possible Russian responses.

*Russians continue their advance.* In the game, the Russians were dispersed and moving rapidly, so the damage to their forces from NATO's nuclear attack had not been substantial. The Russians knew that if their forces continued to advance, additional NATO nuclear attacks on those forces would quickly become impossible without inflicting damage and casualties that the Baltic and other NATO governments would consider unacceptable. Thus, they reasoned, attacks on their forces that would prevent Russia's success were unlikely. Moreover, continuing Russia's rapid advance to the Baltic capitals would present NATO with a situation in which the Russians had succeeded in achieving their aims and NATO would have lost, despite NATO's use of nuclear weapons. The Russians, surrounding or occupying the Baltic capitals and not having responded with nuclear weapons to NATO's first use, could shift the blame to NATO by labeling the Alliance as having engaged in a reckless provocation to which Russia wisely did not respond. The participants considered this response by Russia to be a definite possibility but did not rule out that Russia would find it necessary to respond with a nuclear attack (as in the second two options).

*Russia escalates strongly by conducting nuclear attacks on many NATO targets.* Although the participants believed that this option was a possibility, they considered it to be unlikely because the damage done by the NATO attacks was not substantial and had not affected Russia's ability to achieve its goals. And, because NATO did not conduct the attacks on Russian soil, the participants believed that attacks by Russia on targets in the United States were unlikely.

*Russia responds in kind.* Participants considered this option likely. There were several NATO targets that Russia could attack and cause considerable damage to NATO's air campaign, which was the core of the Alliance's operations and ability to reduce Russian forces—until much, much later, when NATO could, in principle, mount a counterattack. Moreover, there were lucrative targets for Russia to attack with nuclear weapons and damage NATO's ability to mount that counterattack.

To elaborate on the participants' reasoning, we provide the following an example: Stealthy F-22s and F-35s were flying from bases in Europe (e.g., Aviano, Italy; Ramstein, Germany) and were the only aircraft able to attack advancing Russian forces (albeit standing off to some extent because of Russian IADSs). Those aircraft would also play a critical role in causing attrition to the IADSs after the Russians took the Baltic capitals as NATO prepared to launch a counterattack. Damaging or destroying those bases, which are generally not strongly hardened against nuclear attack, would therefore deny NATO critical warfighting capabilities. NATO command and control and air operations centers (e.g., Uedem, Germany) were also generally not hardened against nuclear attack and represented lucrative targets, although NATO might make some use of remote air operations centers. Ports that serve military resupply (e.g., Bremerhaven, Germany) would also be attractive targets, and their destruction would substantially increase the time and complexity required for NATO to mount a counterattack. Reinforcements flowing from the United States would need to use alternative ports, and allied countries might reassess their willingness to receive U.S. forces as a nuclear conflict unfolds.[9]

To be sure, nuclear attacks on these targets would cause substantial numbers of NATO civilian casualties and fatalities (e.g., a 50-kiloton nuclear warhead optimized to 20 pounds per square inch, aiming at aircraft parking areas, might result in more than 5,000 deaths and more than 15,000 casualties). Attacks on other, less likely NATO targets in more-populated areas—such as Izmir, Turkey, or Monsanto, Portugal—could produce deaths and casualties that are ten to 100 times larger. Although participants considered

---

[9] Many of the Russian attacks considered were designed to affect military potential and political will to continue the fight over the longer term. The destruction of aircraft; command, control, communications, computers, and intelligence installations; and other such immediate power projection forces reflected concern over the vulnerability of the Russian forces and could be executed with moderate levels of collateral damage. Attacks against reception locations (e.g., ports) make sense later in the conflict, especially when U.S. forces begin to arrive; at that point, Russia could destroy both the port facilities and the arriving U.S. heavy forces at the same time.

such attacks to be unlikely, population densities around some NATO sites are nonetheless unfavorable.

In our wargame exercise, in response to the NATO attack on its forces, Russia responded in kind by attacking five NATO air bases supporting F-22s, F-35s, or both. It used five moderate-yield nuclear weapons (50-kiloton warheads allowing coverage of key target areas and surrounding areas with support elements dispersed only for protection against conventional attack). The participants then discussed how NATO would respond to Russia's actions and found no good options. As noted earlier, if nuclear exchanges continued, NATO would suffer substantially greater damage to its warfighting capabilities and civilian populations after each exchange than Russia would, unless NATO attacked Russian population centers, which would almost certainly spark dramatic escalation by Russia. At this point, the only military targets that NATO could attack without inflicting substantial damage on the Baltic states would be inside Russia, thereby risking a nuclear exchange that could include Russian attacks on military targets in the United States. As discussed earlier, the participants considered it very unlikely that NATO would choose courses fraught with such dangerous escalatory possibilities. However, regardless of whether NATO attacked military targets in Russia, the participants concluded that NATO lacks escalation dominance—that is, further use of NSNW would only increase NATO's disadvantages relative to Russia—and would likely seek war termination. In the game, NATO's first use of NSNW was essentially a bluff that the Russians called. Ultimately, Russia enjoyed escalation dominance.

### NATO Uses NSNW in Response to Russian First Use

The wargame exercise also considered a case in which the Russians succeeded in their initial invasion into the Baltic states. NATO, which had not employed nuclear weapons, then decided to prepare a counterattack. As U.S. forces flowed into the theater and other NATO forces were mobilized, NATO used F-22s and F-35s to attack Russian air defenses and ground forces with precision munitions that attrite Russian air defenses and ground forces. Although it was not discussed during the game, existing inventories of these weapons are quite limited, which would severely limit the pace and duration of those attacks. Russia became concerned about its force attrition, so it decided to employ nuclear weapons against five NATO air bases supporting operations by the F-22s and F-35s.

As in the previous case, NATO's losses in combat capabilities were significant. The nuclear attack destroyed unique combat and support capabilities that could not be quickly or easily replaced. It degraded NATO's ability to continue attacks on Russian forces in preparation for a counterattack. NATO's abilities to defend its counterattacking forces against Russian air attacks and to provide airborne support were also degraded. This was a significant loss for many reasons, including NATO's lack of robust ground-based and mobile air defense capabilities that could otherwise compensate for the loss of the F-22s and F-35s. The response options that NATO had were essentially the same as those discussed in the NATO first-use case. NATO could not use nuclear weapons against dispersed Russian forces, which were by then in and around the Baltic capitals, without substantial civilian losses and damage to infrastructure. Limited NATO nuclear attacks on targets inside Russia were possible but—as in the other case—risked a strong escalatory response. Furthermore, such attacks would not cause damage substantially affecting Russia's military operations in the Baltic states. Russia, on the other hand, could continue conducting limited nuclear strikes on NATO targets where the attacks would substantially degrade or cripple NATO's ongoing air operations and preparations for counterattack. These tactical nuclear attacks would also cause substantial numbers of civilian casualties and deaths, which NATO governments would find difficult to justify and sustain. Game participants again concluded that NATO threats to escalate to widespread attacks on targets in Russia and general nuclear war were not credible.

## Synopsis of Insights from the Wargame Exercise and Related Analysis

The biggest takeaway from the wargame exercise is that NATO lacks escalation dominance, and Russia has the benefit of it.[10] In contemplating war in the Baltic states, once nuclear attacks commence, NATO would have much stronger military incentives to terminate nuclear operations, if not all of its operations, than Russia would. Significantly, this problem will not be solved by new means of basing or delivery of low-yield nuclear weapons alone, which were assumed to be available to NATO in the exercise. NATO's infrastructure is vulnerable, and damage to it caused by even limited numbers of nuclear attacks can substantially degrade NATO's military capabilities; meanwhile, Russia is able to withstand comparable levels of nuclear strikes against its forces. Russian forces in or around the Baltic capitals would be protected against attack because of their locations, as well as by Russian IADSs. Attacks on Russian logistical or other support inside Russia would entail large numbers of nuclear weapons and risk a strong response against a wide variety of targets that, in the cycle of strike and counterstrike, will tend to favor the Russians, at least in terms of affecting military capabilities in the short term. Even if it chose not to escalate to general war or conduct a wider attack on targets throughout Europe, Russia could continue limited attacks on lucrative NATO military targets. The problem, then, is that NATO lacks the conventional forces required to slow or stop the rapid Russian advance. NSNW forces alone cannot substitute for NATO's lack of those conventional forces.

---

[10] This is a statement about military capabilities, not overall incentives. Given the huge stakes involved, Russia's economic limitations, and international attitudes, Russia may be deterred for broader reasons. Even so, circumstances change and motivations for aggression could rise. Thus, Russia's military-based escalation dominance in the region is an important concern.

CHAPTER SEVEN

# Conclusions

In this chapter, we describe the two general viewpoints of nuclear deterrence (doves and hawks), the implications for theories of victory, other general conclusions from our analysis of NATO nuclear options to deter Russian aggression in the Baltic states, and possible topics for future analysis.

## Two Views of Deterrence

Our review of the nuclear-deterrence literature indicates that there are two views of deterrence—doves and hawks (see Table 2.1). These views have distinct characteristics that have been used, often simultaneously, to articulate policy and to design plans and programs. Doves believe that deterrence is predicated on the threat of escalation to general nuclear war. Hawks believe that deterrence depends on the ability to defeat aggression by, at a minimum, precluding the attacker from succeeding with any plausible theory of victory.

The *theory of victory* (i.e., what it takes to achieve deterrence), then, depends on which view of deterrence one subscribes to or considers to be more important. The theory of victory for each view is as follows:

- Doves: Successful deterrence requires assured retaliation—by assuring that any strike by an adversary can and absolutely will (if not after the first, at least at some point) be followed by a devastating response.

- Hawks: Successful deterrence requires being able to defeat aggression at different rungs of the escalation ladder. That defeat might occur at the same level of violence or an escalated level of violence, including a level well short of initiating general nuclear war. The aggressor would fail to succeed, might suffer considerably more damage than the defending country, and would have no escalatory trump cards.

### Theory of Victory If the Threat of Escalation to General Nuclear War Is Key

Suppose first that the threat of escalation to general nuclear war is the key to victory. An overarching issue would be whether Russia considers it credible that NATO is prepared to move to general nuclear war over the Baltic states. If this idea is credible, then NATO's NSNW capabilities are of lesser importance.

If the credibility is lacking, what then? Those conducting our wargame exercise did not regard the threat as credible, particularly if Russia made it clear that it had no intention of expanding its invasion outside the Baltic states. This doubtful credibility would exist in any case, given realities of geography, history, and economics. It is even greater in 2018, however, because of tensions within NATO and because of President Trump's recent criticisms of NATO countries not paying their fair share of NATO costs. Some believe that, as former Undersecretary of State for Political Affairs Nicholas Burns noted, the current environment constitutes "the most serious transatlantic crisis in 70 years, because the Europeans do not believe Trump is fully committed to the European Union, NATO, or the democratic values that are the foundation of the alliance" (Ignatius, 2018).

It is also unclear whether western European governments, including Great Britain and France (which have nuclear arsenals), would be willing to entertain (even in declaratory statements) such escalation in the absence of attacks on their territory or the expectation of war going beyond the Baltic states. All in all, we do not believe that this view of deterrence makes sense when considering war in the Baltic states.

**Theory of Victory If Defeating Aggression at Different Rungs of the Escalation Ladder Is Key**

Now suppose that the hawks' theory of victory is correct, which seems consistent with the 2018 Nuclear Posture Review's call for "tailored deterrence options" to supplement strategic nuclear options and counter "Moscow's perception that its greater number and variety of non-strategic nuclear systems provide a coercive advantage in crises and at lower levels of conflict" (DoD, 2018, pp. xi–xii).

To explore whether new NSNW could credibly negate such a coercive advantage, our wargame exercise explored the potential military consequences of taking steps up the escalation ladder, assuming that the new NSNW and delivery methods were available. As described earlier, after every sequence of exchanges of NSNW deemed realistic by the players, NATO found itself with greater, if not substantially greater, damage to its ability to conduct warfare than the Russians did, owing to the numerous attractive targets that NATO presents. The conclusion was that new NSNW alone would not change this situation, whatever their number and variety, and would therefore not credibly negate Russian advantages in both NSNW and conventional forces. To put it more bluntly, Russia would still enjoy escalation dominance.

So, what if NATO were to disperse and harden basing to reduce its vulnerabilities and present less-attractive targets? Those steps would still not achieve escalation dominance, particularly if all nuclear strikes (Russian and NATO) occur within NATO countries and thus affect NATO civilian populations. Nuclear attacks launched by either side would be confined to NATO targets unless NATO was willing or felt compelled to risk general nuclear war by attacking targets in Russia. Although NATO could launch such attacks as retaliation for civilian casualties and to demonstrate resolve—potentially causing the Russians to rethink, or even halt, their invasion—attacks on targets inside Russia would do little to prevent Russia from rapidly reaching the Baltic capitals. And if Russia did not halt its operations, NATO would still lack escalation dominance, would have failed to prevent the Russian invasion, and would be in a fraught position while having risked general nuclear war. Moreover, much expensive work would have to be done to harden, disperse, and make NATO's military and military-supporting infrastructure robust. As discussed earlier, costs to achieve those improvements would easily total in the multiple tens of billions of dollars.

## Overall Conclusions

Both views of deterrence (doves and hawks) have played roles, arguably significant and simultaneous, in past policies and plans. Arguably, the threat of general nuclear war has been the most powerful influence on deterrence so far. However, governments have consistently concluded that depending on the threat of Armageddon is unacceptable for security because of the evident problem of limited aggression. During the Cold War, NATO struck a middle course by taking measures to make more credible the possibility that NATO could fight a limited war in Europe but that war would quite possibly escalate, perhaps inexorably, to general nuclear war. After extensive arrangements for nuclear sharing, the entanglement of conventional and nuclear forces, and related doctrinal actions, that credibility was arguably achieved. No comparably credible deterrent exists for defense of the Baltic states. Creating one seems, to us, implausible.

Given this situation, what value might enhancing NATO NSNW have? We see two potential contributions that enhanced NSNW could make:

- denying (or at least diminishing) any perceived unacceptable asymmetries between NATO and Russia in the Baltic region (NATO has political, military, and economic advantages more broadly)
- complicating, perhaps substantially in some cases, Russian calculations of risk and encouraging conservative Russian behavior.

Regarding denying unacceptable asymmetries, some participants in our wargame exercise argued that developing and deploying some number of new NSNW for use by NATO would be prudent. Existing NSNW are inadequate. When arguing for new NSNW, General

Hyten, the commander of U.S. Strategic Command, indicated that (as reflected in our exercise) the limited number of B61 bombs stored at and delivered from a few NATO air bases does not constitute a credible threat "because the aircraft that would deliver [those] bombs, stealthy as they may be, might not be able to get through the Russian air defenses" (Hyten, 2018). Thus, the argument is that the current situation presents an unacceptable asymmetry to NATO: Russia has NSNW that it could credibly use at any time against NATO, while NATO does not have nuclear weapons that it could assuredly use, particularly early in a conflict before its air defenses would be significantly degraded. This asymmetry simplifies Russian decisions to use NSNW. Developing and deploying new, more-survivable weapons might complicate those decisions for Russia. As we demonstrate in Appendix D, developing and acquiring one to several hundred of the new NSNW discussed in the 2018 Nuclear Posture Review would have significant cost—from single-digit billions of dollars to $20 billion, not counting the costs of the command and control and targeting capabilities that would be needed to employ those systems.

In regard to complicating the risk calculus, as discussed in more detail in Appendix A, we see two cases in which having credible NSNW could enhance deterrence during crisis or conflict:

- Russia has invaded without taking risks seriously because of a belief that it can win easily, quickly, and without major adverse international consequences, but the invasion is proceeding badly, inconsistent with those assumptions. In that case, NATO nuclear use, even if demonstrative and not backed up by warfighting capability, might cause a Russian decision to terminate war without necessarily winning.
- Russian thinkers are very cautious about not getting even close to war with NATO, consider various nuclear options for use in conflict, do so making conservative assumptions (i.e., looking at worse-than-expected developments), and conclude that the course of war would be painful and perhaps slow and uncertain. In that case, NATO's possession of NSNW that it could credibly use would reinforce the possibility of further escalation with dire

consequences; thus, cautious Russians would be deterred from invading.

When could these deterrence-favorable cases arise? We see the following as necessary conditions:

- NATO forces must be sized and postured to have the capabilities needed to mount significant resistance to a Russian invasion.
- Russia must not be able to achieve a surprise fait accompli.
- NATO must have battle-competent forces in place when war starts, thereby requiring early decisions and maneuver. Because politically complex reactions to warning are notoriously difficult, this probably implies the need for basing ground forces in the Baltic states rather than counting on the ability to move them from Germany or Poland.
- Any NATO nuclear use must occur *before* Russia succeeds militarily or regards victory as imminent (that is, within hours or a day, not a week).

To achieve these conditions, NATO would need to consider

- substantially enhancing and improving its conventional forces based in and near the Baltic states
- fielding some limited NSNW options feasible for use throughout a conflict, including very early in the conflict[1]
- going through the lengthy and difficult political and military peacetime processes necessary to make prompt response to warning feasible and credible.

We are under no illusions about these steps being easy to execute. And, unfortunately, it will remain the case that if Russia's leadership is aware of and has soberly accepted risks before invasion, a NATO escalation with NSNW would very likely be ineffective. Russia enjoys escalation dominance.

---

[1] For insightful discussion on "nuclear supplements," see Durkalec, 2018, pp. 13–17.

## Possible Topics for Future Analysis

We see our effort as a first step in addressing the many complex issues associated with deterring Russian threats to the Baltic states. We see many topics that merit further study, including the following (some of which could already be underway within NATO):

- What would be an action plan to develop and practice rapid-decision and rapid-action processes to prevent a surprise fait accompli, despite major deception operations by Russia (e.g., plausible exercises)? How much would it cost to execute such a plan? What political challenges would need to be overcome to enable its adoption and assured execution in war? What intelligence, surveillance, and reconnaissance capabilities would be needed to provide the information needed to enable rapid decisionmaking?
- How would gaming change if the initiating scenario resembled the little green men (masked soldiers in unmarked uniforms) employed by Russia in Ukraine in 2014?
- Are there ways that limited nuclear use by NATO could be given significant (although not decisive) military value despite Russian quantitative escalation dominance? What should the objectives be (e.g., to improve the credibility of a demonstration of resolve or to prevent destruction of particular NATO forces)?
- What options exist for geographically horizontal escalation and for escalation into other domains, such as the cyber realm? Are any of these options attractive as possibilities for offsetting Russia's escalation dominance in the nuclear realm?
- Because major reductions of airfield vulnerability would be extremely expensive, what partial measures would be most valuable in terms of raising Russian anxieties about attacking such bases or having confidence in results? Would rotational basing and operations be feasible given the maintenance demands of modern aircraft?
- What infrastructure improvements would be most effective for enabling NATO reinforcement and sustainment of its conven-

tional forces to conduct an opposed counterattack? How much would the improvements cost?

- What, apart from the force options described in this report, would be effective designs for permanently stationed ground forces to be valuable as nontrivial tripwires? How much would those options cost?
- What new capabilities, such as hypersonic weapons, might enable conventional strike options to be effective in blunting a Russian advance in the event that NATO ground forces are *not* in place soon enough to confront Russian invaders? What intelligence, surveillance, and reconnaissance capabilities would be needed to enable the use of those capabilities? How might Russia respond to NATO's deployment of those capabilities? What would be the overall effects of those capabilities on deterrence?
- Other than enhancing their conventional forces, what opportunities, if any, exist for the Baltic nations to put in place steps that would substantially slow a Russian invasion?
- What should be the composition and frequency of NATO exercises that could enhance deterrence? What role should nuclear weapons (including their command and control) play in those exercises? How much would those exercises cost? How can those exercises be structured so as to not provoke Russian fears of a preemptive attack?
- What options are available to counteract the campaigns for nuclear disarmament among NATO populations—which will inevitably continue and be exploited by Russia—if NATO reemphasizes NSNW in its war plans and exercises?

APPENDIX A

# A Deterrence Model for Exploring Issues Speculatively

We developed a model that captures deterrence-related ideas in a superficially rational-actor framework that, notably, allows for effects on limited rationality, such as errors of perception and errors of understanding actual utilities (i.e., those that would be recognized after seeing the consequences of different choices). Although qualitative with no pretense of precision, the model is useful in understanding the dimensions of the deterrence problem and how they interact.[1]

The model illustrates a two-sided situation: Blue uses the model to speculate about whether Red will be deterred. Blue has estimates of how Red views Blue (Red's model of Blue) and of Red's values. Figure A.1 shows the model's inputs, with some illustrative values. On the left side, the inputs specify

- whether, in Blue's judgment, Red will believe that Blue will try to resist invasion
- whether Blue will react fast enough to make such resistance possible
- whether Blue has enhanced its conventional defenses
- whether the capabilities of such enhanced defenses would be nominal or enhanced compared with those in 2018

[1] The model was used internally within the project for thinking about deterrence, was not intended for external use, and has not been subject to verification and validation. The project team determined by inspection that the model correctly reflected the team's qualitative understanding of the issues. The precise numbers are merely illustrative.

**Figure A.1**
**Model Inputs, with Illustrative Values**

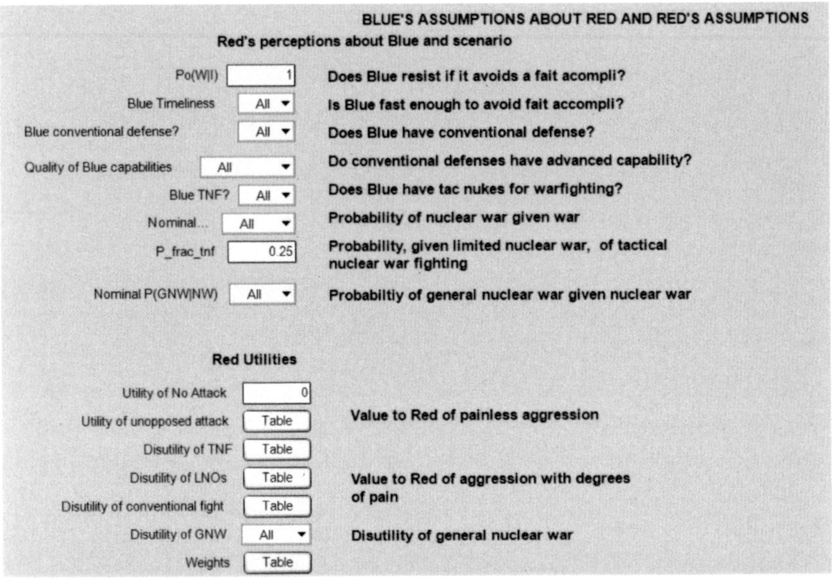


NOTE: GNW = general nuclear war; LNO = limited nuclear option; NW = nuclear war; TNF = tactical nuclear force.

- whether Blue even has tactical nuclear warfighting capabilities
- how likely it is that limited nuclear war would involve tactical use, not just demonstrative use
- how likely it is that a nuclear war would somehow escalate to general nuclear war (the Red planner should recognize that escalation, if it occurs, might be due to Red's leadership rather than Blue's).

On the right side of the model are inputs regarding Red's utilities (as perceived by Blue, which is doing the assessment of deterrence). Not attacking is treated as having a utility value of zero. The other inputs are the assumed Red utility for unopposed aggression and Red disutilities in the event of limited nuclear options, conventional warfare, tactical nuclear warfare, or general nuclear war. As a whole, the model attempts to capture what Red leaders worry about when contemplating invasion: how valuable would a fully successful invasion be, how painful might it be if Blue resisted, how likely are various escalations, and how bad would their consequences be? Real leaders might reason qualitatively or, at best, with fuzzy logic, but the quantitative yet uncertainty-sensitive model allows us to ponder the nature of such reasoning systematically. Furthermore, it can do so while accounting for many departures from sound rational-actor reasoning. For example, misperceptions could cause Red to underestimate or overestimate Blue's willingness to fight and ability to act quickly. Red might irrationally (but sensibly) regard escalation to general nuclear war as more likely than it probably is. Conversely, Red might irrationally treat the probabilities of escalation as zero because humans often ignore possibilities that they see as quite unlikely. Red might also overestimate or underestimate the value of unopposed invasion (e.g., eventual international consequences). Thus, the model can represent parametrically a wide range of nonrational aspects of possible Red reasoning. A more advanced version of the same basic model (not discussed in this report) goes deeper, separately estimating Red's perceptions about most likely, worst-case, and best-case values of key variables.

For every set of input values in Figure A.1, Red is perceived to estimate the utility of invading as an expected utility (on a scale from –1,000 to 1,000) across the set of potential consequences (unopposed war, limited nuclear options, and all the way up through general nuclear war). Figure A.2 shows Red's assumed utilities if Blue fights and has the benefit of strong, advanced conventional defenses.

Red sees the various possibilities for war and computes expected utility by applying probabilities for each escalation.

Figure A.3 illustrates the probability of Red invading, based on this model, as a function of what Red assumes regarding the likelihood of nuclear war (the horizontal axis), the likelihood of such a war becoming general nuclear war (the different curves shown), whether Blue's conventional defenses are strong and advanced (in this case, both, as indicated by the value of "1" for the first input and "advanced" for the fifth input), how bad Red sees general nuclear war being (a disutility of 200), and whether NATO will respond quickly enough to avoid a fait accompli (in this case, yes, as indicated by the value of "1" for the

**Figure A.2**
**Utilities of Possible Wars, as Perceived by Red**

Quality of Blue capabilities: Advanced
Blue Timeliness: 1
Possibilities ☐ Totals
Disutility of GNW ☐ Totals

| | 25 | 50 | 200 | 1000 |
|---|---|---|---|---|
| Unopposed | 50 | 50 | 50 | 50 |
| Conventional Fight | 25 | 25 | 25 | 25 |
| Conv + LNOs | 22 | 22 | 22 | 22 |
| Conv + TNF Fight | 15 | 15 | 15 | 15 |
| GNW | 0 | -25 | -175 | -975 |

timeliness input). The probability of Red invading also is based on a risk-taking model of Red. With these assumptions, if Red believes that the likelihood of general nuclear war is at least one in four if nuclear war occurs (the green curve), then Red will be deterred if it sees war becoming nuclear with more than 50-percent probability. In that case, there would be a 50-percent likelihood that war would become nuclear and a 50-percent likelihood that nuclear war would become general nuclear war, making the probability of general nuclear war 25 percent overall. Given a disutility of 200, that would give a Red invasion a utility of –50, which is the same as the utility of an unopposed invasion.

When using the model, the various inputs can be changed interactively with instantaneous response. Given the same objective circumstances, we might see the following two contrasting Blue models of Red:

- Red 1 is more inclined to believe that Blue would escalate to nuclear use (50-percent chance), believes that any such escalation might escalate to general nuclear war (one in four odds), and sees a large disincentive for general nuclear war (–200, but not negative infinity because Red believes that war would be quickly terminated).

**Figure A.3**
**Probability That Red Will Invade Versus the Probability That War, If It Occurs, Will Become Nuclear**

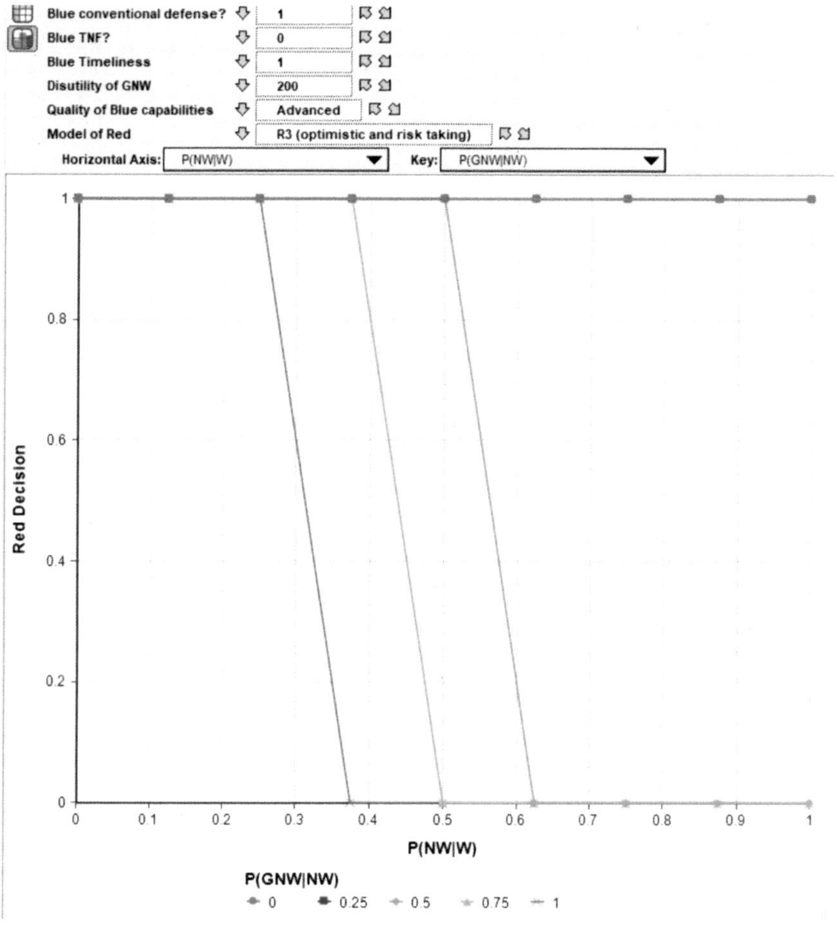


- Red 2 (the model used for Figure A.3) is more contemptuous of Blue, given Blue's inherent military disadvantages resulting from geography; believes that nuclear war is very unlikely (odds less than one in four); and believes that, even if nuclear war occurs, escalation to general nuclear war is similarly unlikely. Thus, this model perceives Red as optimistic and risk-taking.

Table A.1 shows the results using each model of Red. In this case, Blue gets deterrent value for strong conventional defenses, but it gets that value only against Red 1. To be more successful at deterrence, Blue would need to raise Red 2's perceptions of the likelihood of nuclear use, the likelihood that any nuclear use would lead to general nuclear war, or both.

The model is useful for analytic exploration, but the input values drive results. If Red were more rational, deterrence would occur in almost all cases because Red would see the disutility of general nuclear war as having a value of, effectively, negative infinity. Thus, if Red saw *any* nonzero probability of general nuclear war occurring, it would be deterred. Real people, however, sometimes act as though they are *certain* that something will not occur. Also important is the assumption about how much utility Red would see from an unopposed invasion. If Red foresaw great negative international consequences, it would not invade even if it contemplated that Blue would not resist.

## Implications

Using the results from our informal exploratory analysis with the qualitative model and from the wargame exercise described in Chapter Six, we developed a structure for characterizing when upgrades to limited nuclear options might plausibly be effective in helping reestablish

**Table A.1**
**Red's Decision as a Function of Blue's Model of Red**

| | Model of Red | |
|---|---|---|
| **Blue Defenses** | **Red 1** | **Red 2** |
| Current (2018) conventional defenses | Invade | Invade |
| Strong but nominal conventional defenses | Invade | Invade |
| Strong, enhanced conventional defenses | Do not invade | Invade |

deterrence and, thus, what capabilities for such options might be most valuable. The results are shown in Tables A.2 and A.3. Again, these are unabashedly qualitative and judgmental. The table shows our assessment of the value for deterrence of either a small upgrade to NATO's capability for limited nuclear options or a much larger upgrade. The rows specify different cases. As in the rest of the appendix, the intent is to account for different ways the Russians may be thinking. In both of the scenarios illustrated (wartime and peacetime), the cost to NATO of adding a small upgrade is $10 billion, and the cost of adding a larger upgrade is $30 billion.

In Table A.2, we evaluate the value of NATO's limited nuclear options in a war. The biggest distinction among cases is whether Russia had (1) entered the war after recognizing risks, decided to invade

**Table A.2**
**Value of Upgrades to NATO's Nuclear Options for Reestablishing Deterrence During Wartime**

| Context and Russia's Expectation of Events | Value of Small Upgrade to Limited Nuclear Options | Value of Large Upgrade to Limited Nuclear Options |
|---|---|---|
| Context: Russia recognized risks and decided to invade anyway | | |
| Russia's expectation of events | | |
| Quick, easy | None | None |
| Painful, but victory may be imminent | None | None |
| Slow, painful, uncertain outcome | Significant | Significant + |
| Context: Russia greatly underestimated risks and is now eager to avoid broader war | | |
| Russia's expectation of events | | |
| Quick, easy | None | None |
| Painful, but victory may be imminent | Moderate | Moderate |
| Slow, painful, uncertain outcome | High | High |

NOTE: The scale of values in this table is as follows: none, moderate, significant, significant +, high.

anyway, and was prepared to deal with possible difficulties (first set of rows) or (2) invaded without taking risks seriously because of a belief that it could win easily, quickly, and without major adverse international consequences (second set of rows). Within these two contexts, distinctions are drawn based on how—at the time of NATO nuclear use—the war is going from Russia's perspective. The better cases for NATO are in the second context: Russia underestimated or avoided risks, has no taste for larger war, and has had troubles in the invasion. Perhaps Russia's military commanders still assure leadership that victory is imminent (but can their judgment be trusted?), or perhaps they are admittedly uncertain and anticipate slow and painful progress (last row). In those circumstances, NATO nuclear use—even if demonstrative and not backed up by warfighting capability—might cause a Russian decision to terminate war without necessarily winning. Interestingly, it would probably not help much if NATO had made large upgrades to its nuclear capability (third column) because, as we discussed in the main report, even a large increase in NATO's NSNW capability would still leave it inferior to Russia's for warfighting.

The more evident insight from Table A.2 is more sobering. If Russia's leadership had been aware of the risks from the outset, a NATO escalation with NSNW would very likely be ineffective because Russia enjoys escalation dominance. It could win by continuing until its invasion was complete.

Table A.3 is our attempt to map the results from Table A.2 to the peacetime context: Would upgrades to NSNW options help deterrence generally? In the second context of a peacetime evaluation, Russian thinkers are very cautious about not getting even close to war with NATO, consider various nuclear options for use in conflict, do so making conservative assumptions (i.e., looking at worse-than-expected developments), and conclude that the course of war would be painful (and perhaps slow and uncertain).

Again, then, this is the corner of the scenario space in which some upgrades to NATO NSNW capabilities would be valuable. How much value the capabilities would have thus depends on the plausibility of those cases.

**Table A.3**
**Value of Upgrades to NATO's Nuclear Options for Reestablishing Deterrence During Peacetime**

| Context and Russia's Expectation of Events | Value of Small Upgrade to Limited Nuclear Options | Value of Large Upgrade to Limited Nuclear Options |
|---|---|---|
| Context: Russian leaders do cold calculations and will take some risks | | |
| Russia's expectation of events (if Russia invades) | | |
| Quick, easy | None | None |
| Painful, but with relatively quick victory | None | None |
| Slow, painful, uncertain outcome | Significant | Significant + |
| Context: Russian leaders do not want to even get close to war with NATO | | |
| Russia's worst expectation of events (if Russia invades) | | |
| Quick, easy | None | None |
| Painful, but with relatively quick victory | Moderate | Moderate |
| Slow, painful, uncertain outcome | High | High |

NOTE: The scale of values in this table is as follows: none, moderate, significant, significant +, high.

For those deterrence-favorable cases to arise, we see it as necessary that Red believe the following:

1. NATO forces will mount significant resistance to a Russian invasion.
   a. Russia will not be able to do a surprise fait accompli or succeed via use of little green men or other such tactics.
   b. NATO will have battle-competent forces in place when war starts, thereby requiring early decisions and maneuver. (Because politically complex reactions to warning are notoriously difficult, this probably would correspond to NATO having ground forces in the Baltic states rather than counting on the ability to move them from Germany or Poland.)

3. NATO's conventional forces can slow Russia's progress and cause significant pain.
4. NATO's nuclear use, if it occurs, will occur before Russia succeeds militarily or regards victory as imminent (i.e., within hours or a day, not a week).

These necessary conditions suggest that NATO should consider (1) substantially improving its conventional forces for a defense of the Baltic states, (2) fielding some limited NSNW options feasible for use throughout a conflict, and (3) going through the lengthy and difficult political and military peacetime processes necessary to make prompt response to warning feasible and credible (e.g., with tripwire forces in the Baltic states and procedures for rapid decisionmaking). We are under no illusions about these efforts being easy. However, the difficulty will depend on future Russia-NATO relations and other factors.

Regarding NSNW in particular, we do not disagree with the idea expressed in the 2018 Nuclear Posture Review (DoD, 2018) that there could well be a need for new systems that would preclude Russia from having perceived asymmetric advantages. Various aspects of military balances matter to international and domestic perceptions, as well as to the stability of domestic political processes. They sometimes matter more in the realm of perceptions than in the realm of military usefulness. However, whether the specific NSNW systems proposed in the Nuclear Posture Review are the ones that should be pursued is a matter beyond the scope of our assessment.

# Format for Wargaming a Conflict in the Baltic States

R-FLEX is a game format designed to explore complex and somewhat ill-defined problems using a combination of physical gaming elements, including a map with hexagonal grid, counters to represent forces, human adjudicators, a rule set governing interactions within the game (derived from more-detailed analysis and simulation when available), and dice to account for stochastic events when desired.[1] Examples of these elements are shown in Figure B.1. Where analysis is not available, expert elicitation is used to provide a basis for greater refinement before, during, and after the game. In this system, the adjudication is done in the open, with players providing additional information and contributing to learning through the adjudication process. The game

**Figure B.1**
**Illustrative R-FLEX Map and Counters**

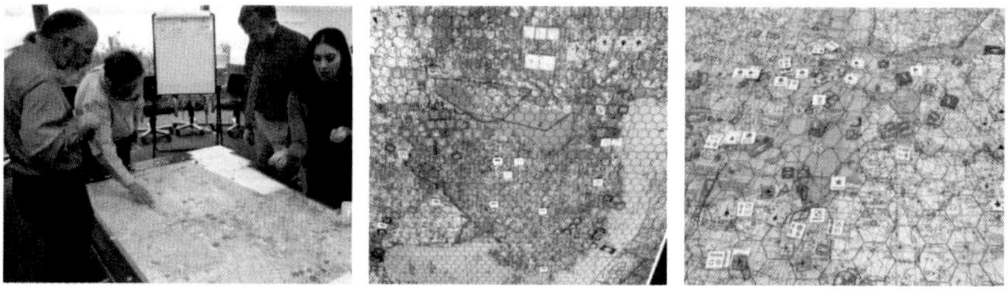

[1] For a description of this framework, see RAND Corporation, 2016.

considers nuclear weapon effects on particular targets, including collateral damage and, as appropriate, civilian casualties and deaths.

R-FLEX–Baltics(N) is a modified R-FLEX game that adds nuclear weapon effects to a scenario in the Baltic states. The game includes adjudication mechanisms accounting for the range of prompt nuclear effects against a variety of targets, including military forces operating in the field, fixed military targets, fallout modeling, and no-strike zones for nuclear weapon use based on various collateral damage constraints. As has been done in the past, the game generally considered brigade-level units (while nonetheless assuming dispersion at lower levels to protect against nuclear attack) to decrease the amount of map clutter. This approach reflects reality, given the tendency of units on both sides to operate together to get benefits from tactical air defenses and to have sufficient firepower to survive a powerful enemy unit that might engage them.

The scenarios examined in the wargame exercise that we conducted (see Chapter Six) made use of the combat adjudication elements, including various air combat, suppression of enemy air defenses, destruction of enemy air defenses, and air-to-ground and army fires rules. The ground movement elements were key to understanding time and space issues, including the ability of the ground forces to spread out, avoid unnecessary contact with opposing forces, move under concealment, and close in on objectives or other sensitive areas to decrease the likelihood of attack by nuclear forces. The game allowed for varying amounts of player interaction, but the focus was on the nuclear-related issues rather than the other command decisions associated with overall war. In particular, the players focused their attention on the overall progression of the war and its interactions with their decisions on nuclear weapon use.

The players used a set of aids to assist in decisionmaking and understanding the scope and nature of the nuclear weapon effects within the context of the game. Examples of the tools used in the exercise are shown in Figure B.2. The player aids focused on, for example, nuclear weapon effects against several different target classes (airfields and forces in road match) (upper left portion of the figure), fallout impact both geographically and on personnel (upper right), and tar-

## Figure B.2
## Illustrative R-FLEX–Baltics(N) Player Aids

### Nuclear Weapons Effects

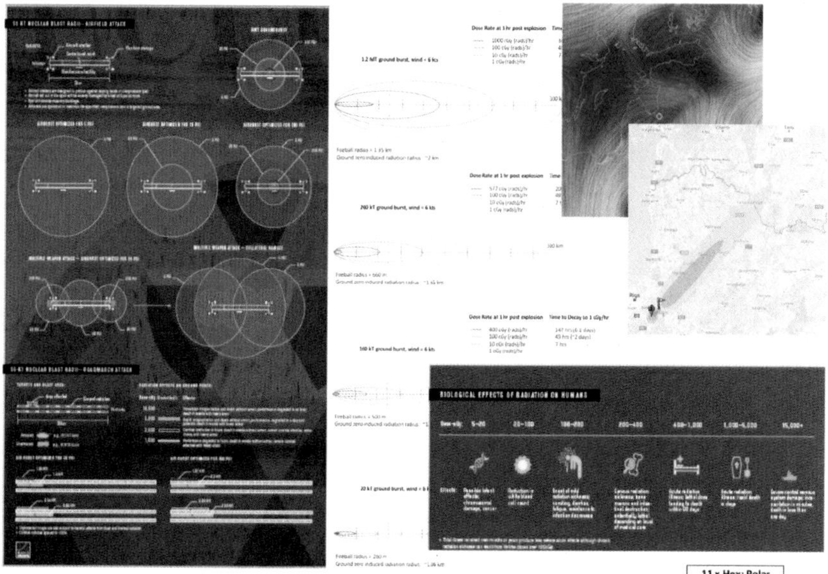

| 11 x Hex; Polar | |
|---|---|
| # MPAs | Pk |
| 0 | 0.0000 |
| 1 | 0.1375 |
| 2 | 0.2561 |
| 3 | 0.3583 |

**Longer Term Radioactive Doses by Day and Week** (cGy)

| Rate at 1 hr (cGy/hr) | Dose in Day 1 | Wk 1 | Wk 2 | Wk 3 | Wk 4 | Wk 5 | Wk 6 | Wk 7 |
|---|---|---|---|---|---|---|---|---|
| 1000 | 2954 | 3798 | 258 | 126 | 82 | 60 | 47 | 38 |
| 577 | 1704 | 2191 | 149 | 73 | 47 | 35 | 27 | 22 |
| 400 | 1182 | 1519 | 103 | 50 | 33 | 24 | 19 | 15 |
| 376 | 1111 | 1428 | 97 | 47 | 31 | 23 | 18 | 14 |
| 100 | 295 | 380 | 26 | 13 | 8 | 6 | 5 | 4 |
| 10 | 30 | 38 | 3 | 1 | 0.8 | 0.6 | 0.5 | 0.4 |
| 1 | 3 | 4 | 0.3 | 0.1 | 0.08 | 0.06 | 0.05 | 0.04 |

**Radioactive Material Internal Hazards**
Mostly arising from ingestion (inhalation hazard lower because of fallout particle sizes) and mostly a latent health threat

### Targeting and Combat Operations

geting and combat operations covering potential targets in NATO member states and Russia (lower portion of the figure). The combination of the basic R-FLEX system and this set of player aids enabled the players to focus on when and why nuclear weapons might be employed, to understand the results of their use, and to explore a relatively large set of options for the use of such weapons.

APPENDIX C

# Conventional Force Cost Estimates

This appendix outlines how we estimated the costs of the enhanced conventional force postures for NATO, discussed in Chapter Three. Here, we estimate cost increases relative to the current (as of 2018) posture.

For ease of comparison in this appendix, we reproduce Table 3.2 in Table C.1. As discussed earlier, the table displays the 2018 NATO force posture and two enhanced postures that have the potential to prevent a rapid fait accompli during a Russian invasion of the Baltic states.

**Table C.1**
**Current and Notional Enhanced NATO Force Postures**

| Posture | U.S. Maneuver |
|---|---|
| Current (2018) | 1 ABCT (rotational)<br>1 SBCT (located in Germany)<br>2 IBCT(ABN)s<br>1 SPMAGTF-CR (located in Spain) |
| Enhanced 1 | 3 ABCTs (located in Poland)<br>1 SBCT (located in Germany)<br>2 IBCT(ABN)s<br>1 SPMAGTF-CR (located in Spain) |
| Enhanced 2 | 4 ABCTs (located in Poland)<br>1 SBCT (located in Germany)<br>2 IBCT(ABN)<br>1 SPMAGTF-CR (located in Spain) |

SOURCE: Based on data from Shlapak and Johnson, 2016.
NOTE: These are the conventional force postures assumed for the cost assessments in this appendix.

## Cost Increases Relative to the Current Posture

As can be seen in Table C.1, the differences among the current and enhanced postures are the number of forward-deployed ABCTs. The current posture includes one rotationally deployed ABCT located in Germany. Enhanced 1 shifts this rotational deployment to be forward-deployed and adds two additional forward-deployed ABCTs (three total), all based in Poland. Finally, Enhanced 2 adds a fourth forward-deployed ABCT in Poland to Enhanced 1's three. The relative cost increase is then dictated by the operations and support (O&S) costs for the additional forward-deployed ABCTs.[1]

The remainder of this appendix describes in greater detail the estimated cost differences for each posture, accounting for shifts from rotational to forward deployments and the total ABCT annual O&S costs associated with the latter.

## Rotational Versus Forward Deployment

ABCT annual recurring costs are classified into three primary categories: (1) ABCT O&S costs, (2) O&S costs of enabling units, and (3) additional operational tempo (OPTEMPO) costs to support European and Baltic-specific training exercises. ABCT O&S cost estimates are provided, for example, by Lostumbo et al. (2013) and Deni (2017). Deni (2017) distinguishes between a unit based under U.S. Army Forces Command and one based under U.S. Army Europe—the latter being more expensive. Additional OPTEMPO costs in support of European deterrence activities are estimated to be FY 2017 $496.10 million for rotational deployments and FY 2017 $327.70 million for forward deployments (Deni, 2017). Rotational deployments also incur movement costs to and from theater, which are a function of the deployment frequency. In total, and neglecting cost differences

[1] The formal definition of O&S is given by the Office of Cost Assessment and Program Evaluation in its O&S cost guidance. O&S includes all costs associated with operating a given Army unit, including O&M and military personnel costs. See Office of Cost Assessment and Program Evaluation, 2014.

associated with enabling units, Deni (2017) estimates that rotational deployments are approximately FY 2017 $135 million (or FY 2018 $140 million) more expensive annually than forward deployments.[2]

An additional point of comparison is provided by Lostumbo et al. (2013), which calculates the relative cost difference between personnel who are forward-based and those based in the continental United States. The analysis estimated (1) the recurring annual fixed cost of maintaining a military base in Europe and (2) the recurring annual variable cost per U.S. military personnel based in Europe relative to the same cost per personnel based in the continental United States. The authors also estimated movement costs as a function of rotational deployment frequency. Assuming no base closures or openings from a shift in posture, the difference between rotational and forward deployments is equal to the difference between ABCT movement costs and the increase in cost to forward-deploy ABCT personnel using the variable relative cost multiplier estimated by Lostumbo et al. (2013). This difference yields a cost savings of FY 2018 $50 million by switching from a rotational to a forward-deployed posture.[3]

## Cost of a Forward-Deployed Armored Brigade Combat Team

We compiled estimates for annual O&S costs of a forward-deployed ABCT in Germany or Poland using three sources: Deni (2017), Shlapak and Johnson (2016), and the European Deterrence Initiative budget (Office of the Under Secretary of Defense [Comptroller], 2017, 2018).[4] These estimates provide a combination of ABCT O&S, enabling unit O&S, and additional OPTEMPO costs, as indicated in Table C.2. The estimate generated by Shlapak and Johnson (2016) includes both

---

2 Deni (2017) assumed nine-month rotational deployments.

3 This assumes a nine-month rotational deployment, as in Deni (2017), and that all relevant ABCT equipment is sealifted to Europe.

4 Prior to the FY 2019 budget request, this was known as the European Reassurance Initiative.

**Table C.2**
**Armored Brigade Combat Team Annual Operations and Support Costs, Derived from Multiple Sources**

| Source | ABCT O&S Costs | Enabling Unit O&S Costs | OPTEMPO Costs | Deployment Type | Total Costs (FY 2018 $ millions) |
|---|---|---|---|---|---|
| Deni (2017) | X | | X | Forward | 1,080 |
| Shlapak and Johnson (2016) | X | X | | Forward | 930 |
| European Reassurance Initiative Budget Request FY 2018 | X | X | X | Rotational | 690 |
| European Deterrence Initiative Budget Request FY 2019 | X | X | X | Rotational | 890 |

SOURCES: Deni, 2017; Office of the Under Secretary of Defense (Comptroller), 2017, 2018; Shlapak and Johnson, 2016.

sets of O&S costs for forward-deployed ABCTs. Deni (2017), however, provides only ABCT O&S costs, but that source includes additional OPTEMPO costs associated with increased training exercises and activities. The European Deterrence Initiative budget data are for a single rotational ABCT and include costs for transportation, life support, temporary duty, OPTEMPO, division headquarters, enabling units, and pay for extended training. Totals as reported by each source are given in Table C.2.

We combine the cost elements shown in Table C.2 to generate an estimated total O&S cost for an ABCT, including base and enabling unit O&S and additional OPTEMPO costs. For example, to generate a forward-deployed estimate from the European Deterrence Initiative data, two steps are required.[5] First, the ABCT is shifted from rotational to forward deployment using the average of the estimated cost

[5] Note that additional training costs for Army units (ABCTs, IBCTs, and SBCTs) are included as separate line items in the European Reassurance Initiative and European Deterrence Initiative budgets, implying that these estimated annual O&S costs are underestimates.

savings from the previous section—FY 2018 $95 million. Second, personnel costs for base pay and benefits are added to obtain an estimate of total annual O&S costs.[6] Personnel costs for both an ABCT and enabling units assumed by Shlapak and Johnson (2016) are applied. In the case of the Deni (2017) estimate, the enabling unit O&S costs are added from Shlapak and Johnson (2016). Finally, for the Shlapak and Johnson (2016) estimate, the additional OPTEMPO costs from Deni (2017) are added. In all three cases, the total O&S costs that we estimate are approximately FY 2018 $1.1 billion to $1.3 billion.

Finally, two additional costs can be considered. First, if existing equipment is not repurposed for the additional ABCTs, force posture enhancements will require the acquisition of new systems. Shlapak and Johnson (2016) estimated the total acquisition cost for three new ABCTs and corresponding enabling equipment to be FY 2016 $13 billion, which is approximately scaled to the number of ABCTs in a given enhanced posture. Second, to forward deploy in Poland, additional infrastructure costs will be incurred. Deni (2017) estimated these costs to be on the order of FY 2017 $1 billion to $1.2 billion for a single ABCT. Assuming a cost-sharing arrangement with Poland, this cost could be closer to FY 2017 $550 million. In the worst case, this up-front investment is assumed to scale with the number of forward-deployed ABCTs. We estimated annual O&M costs for these forward bases in Poland from Lostumbo et al. (2013), using that study's estimate of FY 2013 $115 million per year for an Army installation in Europe.

Table C.3 shows estimated cost differences for the enhanced postures relative to the current posture, reflecting up-front costs and five years of annual O&S (i.e., a five-year deployment), both with and without procurement costs. We generated the cost ranges under the assumptions displayed in the table note.

---

[6] According to the O&S cost guidelines from the Office of Cost Assessment and Program Evaluation (2014), base pay is funded out of military personnel funds, and benefits are funded out of both military personnel and O&M funds. The European Deterrence Initiative is funded from overseas contingency operations funds; an examination of Army budget requests indicates that only base pay and benefits for additional Initiative-specific training exercises are funded from the overseas contingency operations fund.

**Table C.3**
**Estimated Cost Increases for Enhanced Force Postures, With and Without Procurement Costs**

| Posture | Cost Increase With Procurement Costs (FY 2018 $ billions) | Cost Increase Without Procurement Costs (FY 2018 $ billions) |
|---|---|---|
| Current (2018) | Baseline | Baseline |
| Enhanced 1 | +18–24 | +8–14 |
| Enhanced 2 | +28–36 | +12–21 |

NOTE: In the range of the displayed costs, the low value neglects personnel costs. The high value includes all estimated costs.

APPENDIX D

# Tactical Nuclear Force Cost Estimates

As part of this study, we estimated costs of the tactical nuclear force using DoD budget data, historical program costs, and estimates of the size of the current nuclear stockpile.[1] The cost estimates here are for research, development, test, and evaluation (RDT&E); unit procurement; and annual O&M costs of new weapon systems and warheads. We did not include any new or additional command and control systems that may be required to properly operate new tactical nuclear weapons or additional security infrastructure needed for warhead storage. We assumed that new weapon systems will make use of existing launchers. The estimates are rough lower bounds for costs to develop, acquire, and maintain new tactical nuclear systems. Personnel costs would increase the total, as would costs for additional operations.

## Costs of New Weapon Systems

For this analysis, we estimated the costs of three warhead-compatible systems: (1) a new cruise missile, similar to the Cold War–era GLCM; (2) a new short-, medium-, or intermediate-range ballistic missile, similar to the Cold War–era Pershing II intermediate-range ballistic missile; and (3) a new tactical variant of the Trident II SLBM as proposed in the 2018 Nuclear Posture Review (DoD, 2018). For simplicity, we

[1] The actual numbers of warheads and detailed cost information of previously developed and acquired tactical nuclear weapons are classified. Thus, this analysis presents estimates based strictly on open-source data.

assumed that the cost of the new cruise missile is invariant to the type of delivery system (air-launched, submarine-launched, or ground-launched). The following sections describe the derivation of these estimates in more detail.

## A New Cruise Missile

We based the cost of a new tactical nuclear cruise missile on the costs of historical cruise missile programs, both nuclear and nonnuclear. Table D.1 displays the compiled data applied in our cost analysis. We based the costs for the GLCM, a Cold War–era tactical nuclear cruise missile maintained by the Air Force, on estimated development and procurement costs from Schwartz (1998) and a U.S. General Accounting Office (GAO; now the U.S. Government Accountability Office) analysis of potential cost reductions associated with ending the GLCM program following the signing of the Intermediate-Range Nuclear Forces Treaty (GAO, 1988). Our estimates for a new ALCM, the Long-Range Stand-Off weapon, were derived from the Congressional Budget Office (CBO)'s recent nuclear force modernization cost analysis (CBO, 2017) and Evans and Schwalbe (2017), both of which estimated RDT&E and average unit costs for the new system. We included two

**Table D.1**
**Estimated Cruise Missile Costs**

| Missile Type | Year | RDT&E Costs (FY 2018 $ millions) | Average Unit Costs (FY 2018 $ millions) | Annual O&M Costs (FY 2018 $ millions) |
|---|---|---|---|---|
| GLCM | 1977 | 660 | 10.5 | 0.40 |
| Long-Range Stand-Off weapon | New | 3,500–4,000 | 4–9 | — |
| TLAM Block IV | 1974 | 900 | 1.5 | 0.03 |
| AGM-86B | 1985 | 3,000 | 1.1 | 0.04 |
| AGM-129 | 1998 | — | 6.9 | — |

SOURCES: Based on data from CBO, 2017; Department of the Air Force, 2017; Department of the Navy, 2016; DoD, 2017; Evans and Schwalbe, 2017; GAO, 1988; Schwartz, 1998.

NOTE: — indicates that data were not available.

additional ALCMs in our assessment: (1) the AGM-86B, which is the nuclear variant of an ALCM developed in the 1970s, and (2) the AGM-129, or Advanced Cruise Missile, which is another nuclear warhead–compatible platform that has since been deactivated. RDT&E and unit costs were provided by or estimated from Schwartz (1998) and available Air Force cost data. We obtained annual O&M costs for the AGM-86B from Air Force budget data (Department of the Air Force, 2017), given that the platform is still in service. Finally, we included the TLAM in our analysis, given that a nuclear variant was proposed in the 2018 Nuclear Posture Review. We estimated RDT&E and unit costs using the most recently available Selected Acquisition Report for the TLAM Block IV (DoD, 2017) and obtained annual O&M costs from recent Navy budget requests (Department of the Navy, 2016).

We used the costs compiled in Table D.1 to define the estimated cost ranges for a new cruise missile platform, along with similar ranges developed for a new short-, medium-, or intermediate-range ballistic missile and SLBM (discussed in the next two sections); these values are shown in Table D.4 later in this appendix. In defining these cost ranges, we increased RDT&E and unit cost data drawn from historical programs by 10 percent for every decade between initial program development start to 2018 to reflect real cost growth, given increased capability and technological complexity. This approach follows the methods applied by CBO in its estimates for new nuclear weapon programs. Finally, Table D.4 also includes estimates of the number of military personnel required per GLCM and short-, medium-, or intermediate-range ballistic missile. We derived these from a GAO analysis that estimated the manpower reductions associated with the removal of GLCMs and Pershing IIs from Europe immediately following the signing of the Intermediate-Range Nuclear Forces Treaty (GAO, 1989).

### A New Short-, Medium-, or Intermediate-Range Ballistic Missile

We based the cost of a new tactical ballistic cruise missile on the costs of two historical ballistic missile programs—the nuclear-compatible Pershing II and the MGM-140 Army Tactical Missile System (a short-range ballistic missile). Table D.2 displays the compiled data used in our cost analysis.

**Table D.2**
**Estimated Ballistic Missile Costs**

| Missile Type | Year | RDT&E Costs (FY 2018 $ millions) | Average Unit Costs (FY 2018 $ millions) | Annual O&M Costs (FY 2018 $ millions) |
|---|---|---|---|---|
| Pershing II | 1975 | 1,200 | 13.0 | 0.6 |
| MGM-140 Army Tactical Missile System | 1978 | 1,200 | 1.0 | — |

SOURCES: Based on data from DoD, 2002; GAO, 1988, 1989; Schwartz, 1998.
NOTE: — indicates that data were not available.

We derived our cost estimates for the Pershing II, a Cold War–era tactical nuclear intermediate-range ballistic missile maintained by the Army, on data drawn from Schwartz (1998) and GAO (1988, 1989). We obtained data for the MGM-140 Army Tactical Missile System from the most recently available Selected Acquisition Report (DoD, 2002), but annual O&M costs could not be found in recent Army budget requests. Therefore, we estimated the lower bound on annual O&M costs using the same percentage of average unit procurement costs as for the TLAM Block IV cruise missile—that is, approximately 2 percent. Assumed cost ranges are displayed in Table D.4.

### A New Tactical Submarine-Launched Ballistic Missile

We estimated the cost of a new tactical SLBM (i.e., tactical Trident II) using data from CBO (2017); development costs are shown in Table D.3. However, because a new SLBM will be developed in the coming years, we do not include these costs in our analysis because we assume that the cost of repurposing one of these missiles for tactical use will be small relative to the total development cost. In addition, we assumed the unit procurement cost for the new missile to be the same as the old missile, even though the tactical variant will carry only a single warhead. We estimated O&M costs using Navy budget requests for ballistic missile support on board the 14 U.S. nuclear-powered ballistic missile submarines (Department of the Navy, 2016). We derived a unit O&M cost assuming 28 Trident IIs per vessel. We obtained the

**Table D.3**
**Estimated Submarine-Launched Ballistic Missile Costs**

| Missile Type | Year | RDT&E Costs (FY 2018 $ millions) | Average Unit Costs (FY 2018 $ millions) | Annual O&M Costs (FY 2018 $ millions) |
|---|---|---|---|---|
| SLBM | New | 18,400 | 84 | 3.2 |

SOURCES: Based on data from CBO, 2017; Department of the Navy, 2016.

O&M lower bound shown in Table D.4 by again assuming 2 percent of the average unit procurement cost, as estimated from cruise missile O&M costs in Table D.1.

## Costs of New Warheads

Program costs for warhead development and procurement are classified. As a result, we estimated the unit cost for a new warhead from the corresponding Life Extension Programs and estimates of the size of the current U.S. nuclear stockpile. Life Extension Program budget data are available from the U.S. Department of Energy and the National Nuclear Security Administration budget requests and, when available, Selected Acquisition Reports. Our estimates of the nuclear stockpile come from Schwartz (1998), Norris and Kristensen (2011), and Kristensen and Norris (2014). Note that, because Life Extension Programs are ongoing, we considered their RDT&E costs to be sunk and thus did not include them in this analysis.

### A New B61 Warhead

As discussed in Chapter Four, the B61 warhead is currently undergoing a Life Extension Program to consolidate several variants into the B61-12, an air-launched gravity bomb. Given that there are some B61s currently stored in Europe, updating these warheads could be included as a cost if they are ultimately deployed in support of the Baltic states. Table D.5 shows the unit costs that we estimated from the Life Extension Program budget data and O&M costs that we derived from Department of Energy and National Nuclear Security Admin-

**Table D.4**
**Ranges of Estimated Costs for Three New Tactical Nuclear Weapon Systems**

| Missile Type | Total RDT&E Costs (FY 2018 $ millions) | | | Procurement Costs per System (FY 2018 $ millions) | | | Annual O&M Costs per System (FY 2018 $ millions) | | | Number of Military Personnel per System | | |
|---|---|---|---|---|---|---|---|---|---|---|---|---|
| | Low | Middle | High | Low | Middle | High | Low | Middle | High | Low | Middle | High |
| GLCM | 930 | 2,500 | 3,800 | 2.0 | 6 | 15 | 0.04 | 0.2 | 0.4 | 15 | 22 | 28 |
| Short-, medium-, or intermediate-range ballistic missile | 1,200 | 1,700 | 2,200 | 1.5 | 10 | 19 | 0.02 | 0.3 | 0.6 | 21 | 30 | 39 |
| SLBM | | 18,400 | | | 84 | | 2.00 | | 3.0 | | | |

istration budget requests for stockpile management. Note that the B61 Life Extension Program includes a DoD program to develop and install a new tail kit to improve delivery accuracy (see DoD, 2013a, 2016, 2017; U.S. Department of Energy, 2017).

### A New W80 Warhead

The W80 warhead has been previously used on nuclear cruise missiles, such as the GLCM, ALCM, and Advanced Cruise Missile (AGM-129). We estimated the W80's unit and O&M costs analogously to our estimates of the B61's costs, and the resulting cost ranges are given in Table D.5. In this analysis, we assumed the W80 to be the warhead for new cruise missile and short-, medium-, or intermediate-range ballistic missile platforms. Table D.5 also shows the nominal estimates for the sizes of current stockpiles that we assumed when deriving cost ranges.

### A New W76 Warhead

The W76 warhead is currently used aboard the Trident II, and a new low-yield variant, the so-called W76-2, has been proposed for use aboard a new tactical Trident II SLBM, as discussed earlier. Its estimated unit and O&M costs are also given in Table D.5, with the former derived from the corresponding Selected Acquisition Report (DoD, 2013b).

**Table D.5**
**Ranges of Estimated Costs for Three New Tactical Nuclear Warheads**

| | Procurement Costs per Warhead (FY 2018 $ millions) | | | Total O&M Costs per Warhead (FY 2018 $ millions) | | | |
|---|---|---|---|---|---|---|---|
| Warhead | Low | Middle | High | Low | Middle | High | Number in U.S. Stockpile |
| B61 | 6 | 8 | 11 | 0.09 | 0.10 | 0.20 | 500 |
| W80 | 2 | 3 | 4 | 0.07 | 0.09 | 0.10 | 825 |
| W76 | 1 | 2 | 3 | 0.02 | 0.03 | 0.04 | 1,600 |

SOURCES: Based on data from DoD, 2013a, 2013b, 2016, 2017; U.S. Department of Energy, 2017.

NOTE: The ranges are due to uncertainties in the size of the current U.S. stockpile for each type of warhead.

## Illustrative Cost Analysis

We used the cost ranges in Table D.4 to estimate the total cost of an example of a newly acquired tactical nuclear force. The parameters assumed in this example are given in Table D.6, and results are presented in Table D.7. Note that personnel costs are estimated only for the new cruise missile and short-, medium-, or intermediate-range ballistic missile platforms, given available data from GAO (1989); we assumed that new Army and Air Force personnel will be required to operate these platforms. As a result, we assumed the average total cost of base pay and benefits as estimated by CBO (2012). In addition, these costs do not include O&M and personnel costs associated with operating delivery platforms (e.g., the F-35 for air-delivering B61s). CBO, for example, has previously assumed some fraction of missions dedicated to nuclear-related activities for relevant weapon systems, but, given our lack of detailed budget data, we do not make that assumption in our analysis.

**Table D.6**
**Parameters Assumed in an Illustrative Tactical Nuclear Cost Analysis**

| System | Warhead | Number in Illustrative Force |
|---|---|---|
| F-35-delivered B61 | B61 | 200 |
| Cruise missile | W80 | 150 |
| Intermediate-range ballistic missile | W80 | 150 |
| SLBM | W76 | 100 |

**Table D.7**
**Estimated Costs for an Illustrative Tactical Nuclear Force**

| | Total RDT&E, Procurement, and O&M Costs (FY 2018 $ billions) | Personnel Costs (FY 2018 $ billions) | Total Costs (FY 2018 $ billions) |
|---|---|---|---|
| Illustrative tactical nuclear force (Table D.6) | 17–23 | 3.5–5 | 21–27 |

NOTE: Costs include five years of operational deployment.

# References


AECOM, *Rail Baltica: Final Report*, Vol. 1, Chelmsford, Essex, UK: Saxon House, May 2011. As of November 7, 2018:
http://www.railbaltica.org/wp-content/uploads/2017/05/AECOM_Final_Report_Volume_I.pdf

Ahmed, Mansoor, *Pakistan's Tactical Nuclear Weapons and Their Impact on Stability*, Carnegie Endowment for International Peace, Washington, D.C., 2016.

Aksenov, O. Y., Y. N. Tret'yakov, and E. N. Filin, "Osnovnye printsipy sozdaniya sistemy otsenki tekushchego i prognoznogo ushcherba vazhneishim ob'ektam sistemy strategicheskogo sderzhivaniya [Basic Principles for Creating a Current and Prospective Damage Assessment System for the Most Important Areas of the Strategic Deterrence System]," *Voennaya Mysl'*, No. 6, June 2015, pp. 68–74.

Andreasen, Steve, Isabelle Williams, Brian Rose, Hans M. Kristensen, and Simon Lunn, *Building a Safe, Secure and Credible NATO Nuclear Posture*, Washington, D.C.: Nuclear Threat Initiative, January 2018.

Arbatov, Alexei, "Yadernii Potolok," VPK News, July 21, 2014. As of August 18, 2018:
http://vpk-news.ru/print/articles/21133

Arkin, William M., and Richard Fieldhouse, *Nuclear Battlefields: Global Links in the Arms Race*, Cambridge, Mass.: Ballinger Publishing, 1985.

Arquilla, John, and Paul K. Davis, *Modeling Decisionmaking of Potential Proliferators as Part of Developing Counterproliferation Strategies*, Santa Monica, Calif.: RAND Corporation, MR-467, 1994. As of August 18, 2018:
https://www.rand.org/pubs/monograph_reports/MR467.html

Bearak, Max, "This Tiny Stretch of Countryside Is All That Separates Baltic States from Russian Envelopment," *Washington Post*, WorldViews, June 20, 2016.

Blank, Stephen J., ed., *Russian Nuclear Weapons: Past, Present, and Future*, Carlisle Barracks, Pa.: Strategic Studies Institute, U.S. Army War College, November 2011.

Bonds, Tim, and Danielle C. Tarraf, "Assessment of System of Systems Enhanced Small Unit (SESU)," briefing to Defense Advanced Research Projects Agency, Santa Monica, Calif.: RAND Corporation, 2017.

Boston, Scott, Michael Johnson, Nathan Beauchamp-Mustafaga, and Yvonne K. Crane, *Assessing the Conventional Force Imbalance in Europe: Implications for Countering Russian Local Superiority*, Santa Monica, Calif.: RAND Corporation, RR-2402, 2018. As of November 12, 2018:
https://www.rand.org/pubs/research_reports/RR2402.html

Bracken, Paul, *The Second Nuclear Age: Strategy, Danger, and the New Power Politics*, New York: Times Books, 2012.

Brodie, Bernard, ed., *The Absolute Weapon: Atomic Power and World Order*, New York: Harcourt Brace and Co., 1946.

———, *Strategy in the Missile Age*, Santa Monica, Calif.: RAND Corporation, CB-137-1, 1959. As of November 7, 2018:
https://www.rand.org/pubs/commercial_books/CB137-1.html

Brown, Harold, "Rebuttal—A Countervailing View: No, We Did Not Think We Could Win a Nuclear War," *Foreign Policy*, September 24, 2012.

Bundy, McGeorge, "Paper Prepared by Thomas C. Schelling, July 5, 1961," in Charles S. Sampson and Glenn W. LaFantasie, eds., *Foreign Relations of the United States, 1961–1963*, Vol. 14: *Berlin Crisis, 1961–1962*, Washington, D.C.: U.S. Department of State, Office of the Historian, 1993.

Burr, William, "Reagan's Nuclear War Briefing, Declassified," Washington, D.C.: National Security Archive Project, George Washington University, 2016.

Butler, George Lee, *Uncommon Cause: A Life at Odds with Convention*, Vol. I: *The Formative Years*, Parker, Colo.: Outskirts Press, 2016a.

———, *Uncommon Cause: A Life at Odds with Convention*, Vol. II: *The Transformative Years*, Parker, Colo.: Outskirts Press, 2016b.

Byrne, Malcolm, ed., *The Battle for Iran, 1953: Re-Release of CIA Internal History Spotlights New Details About Anti-Mosaddeq Coup*, Washington, D.C.: National Security Archive Project, George Washington University, 2014.

CBO—*See* Congressional Budget Office.

Central Intelligence Agency Office of Transnational Issues, "Evidence of Russian Development of New Subkiloton Nuclear Warheads," Intelligence Memorandum, August 30, 2000. As of November 7, 2018:
https://www.cia.gov/library/readingroom/docs/DOC_0001260463.pdf

Chivvis, Christopher S., *Understanding Russian "Hybrid Warfare" and What Can Be Done About It*, testimony before the House Armed Services Committee, Santa Monica Calif.: RAND Corporation, 2017. As of November 7, 2018:
https://www.rand.org/multimedia/video/2017/03/22/understanding-russian-hybrid-warfare.html

Churchill, Winston, "Never Despair," speech, UK House of Commons, London, March 1, 1955. As of November 7, 2018:
https://www.winstonchurchill.org/resources/speeches/1946-1963-elder-statesman/never-despair

Cimbala, Stephen J., *Getting Nuclear Weapons Right: Managing Danger and Avoiding Disaster*, Boulder, Colo: Lynne Rienner, 2018.

Clapper, James R., *Facts and Fears: Hard Truths from a Life in Intelligence*, New York: Penguin Random House, 2018.

Colby, Elbridge, "Countering Russian Nuclear Strategy in Central Europe," Center for a New American Security, November 11, 2015. As of June 14, 2018:
https://www.cnas.org/publications/commentary/countering-russian-nuclear-strategy-in-central-europe

Congressional Budget Office, *Costs of Military Pay and Benefits in the Defense Budget*, Washington, D.C., November 2012. As of May 30, 2018:
https://www.cbo.gov/sites/default/files/112th-congress-2011-2012/reports/11-14-12-militarycomp0.pdf

———, *Approaches for Managing the Costs of U.S. Nuclear Forces, 2017 to 2046*, Washington, D.C., October 2017. As of August 18, 2018:
https://www.cbo.gov/system/files?file=115th-congress-2017-2018/reports/53211-nuclearforces.pdf

Danby, Nick J., "Baltic Peace Through NATO Strength," *International Policy Digest*, July 24, 2018. As of December 5, 2018:
https://intpolicydigest.org/2018/07/24/baltic-peace-through-nato-strength

Davis, Paul K., *Studying First-Strike Stability with Knowledge-Based Models of Human Decision Making*, Santa Monica, Calif.: RAND Corporation, R-3689-CC, 1989. As of August 18, 2018:
https://www.rand.org/pubs/reports/R3689.html

———, "Improving Deterrence in the Post–Cold War Era: Some Theory and Implications for Defense Planning," in Paul K. Davis, ed., *New Challenges for Defense Planning: Rethinking How Much Is Enough*, Santa Monica, Calif.: RAND Corporation, MR-400-RC, 1994, pp. 197–222. As of August 18, 2018:
https://www.rand.org/pubs/monograph_reports/MR400.html

———, "Synthetic Cognitive Modeling of Adversaries for Effects-Based Planning, Modeling Adversaries and Related Cognitive Biases," in Alex F. Sisti and Dawn A. Trevisani, eds., *Proceedings of SPIE: Enabling Technologies for Simulation Science VI*, Vol. 4716, July 2002, pp. 236–250.

———, *Analysis to Inform Defense Planning Despite Austerity*, Santa Monica, Calif.: RAND Corporation, RR-482-OSD, 2014. As of August 18, 2018:
https://www.rand.org/pubs/research_reports/RR482.html

———, *Illustrating a Model-Game-Model Paradigm for Using Human Wargames in Analysis*, Santa Monica, Calif.: RAND Corporation, WR-1179, 2017. As of August 18, 2018:
https://www.rand.org/pubs/working_papers/WR1179.html

Davis, Paul K., and John Arquilla, *Deterring or Coercing Opponents in Crisis: Lessons from the War with Saddam Hussein*, Santa Monica, Calif.: RAND Corporation, R-4111-JS, 1991. As of August 18, 2018:
https://www.rand.org/pubs/reports/R4111.html

Davis, Paul K., and Brian Michael Jenkins, *Deterrence and Influence in Counterterrorism: A Component in the War on al Qaeda*, Santa Monica, Calif.: RAND Corporation, MR-1619-DARPA, 2002. As of August 18, 2018:
https://www.rand.org/pubs/monograph_reports/MR1619.html

Davis, Paul K., Jeongeun Kim, Yunho Park, and Peter A. Wilson, "Deterrence and Stability for the Korean Peninsula," *Korean Journal of Defense Analyses*, Vol. 28, No. 1, 2016, pp. 1–23.

Delpech, Therese, *Nuclear Deterrence in the 21st Century: Lessons from the Cold War for a New Era of Strategic Piracy*, Santa Monica, Calif.: RAND Corporation, MG-1103-RC, 2012. As of August 18, 2018:
https://www.rand.org/pubs/monographs/MG1103.html

Deni, John R., *Rotational Deployments vs. Forward Stationing: How Can the Army Achieve Assurance and Deterrence Efficiently and Effectively?* Carlisle Barracks, Pa.: U.S. Army War College Press, 2017.

Department of the Air Force, *Fiscal Year (FY) 2018 Budget Estimates: Operation and Maintenance, Air Force*, Vol. II, Washington, D.C., May 2017.

Department of the Navy, *Fiscal Year (FY) 2017 Budget Estimates: Operation and Maintenance, Navy (OMN)*, Vol. II: *Data Book*, Washington, D.C., February 2016.

Director of Central Intelligence, *National Intelligence Estimate, 11-3/8-76*, Washington, D.C., 1976. As of November 28, 2018:
https://catalog.archives.gov/id/6924392

DoD—*See* U.S. Department of Defense.

Durkalec, Jacek, *Nuclear-Backed "Little Green Men": Nuclear Messaging in the Ukraine Crisis*, Warsaw: Polish Institute of International Affairs, 2015.

———, *The 2018 U.S. Nuclear Posture Review: NATO's Brussels Summit and Beyond*, Livermore, Calif.: Lawrence Livermore National Laboratory, Center for Global Security Research, June 2018.

Evans, Dennis, and Jonathan Schwalbe, *The Long-Range Standoff (LRSO) Cruise Missile and Its Role in Future Nuclear Forces*, Laurel, Md.: Johns Hopkins University Applied Physics Laboratory, 2017.

Fiott, Daniel, "Modernising NATO's Defence Infrastructure with EU Funds," *Survival*, Vol. 58, No. 2, 2016, pp. 77–94.

Frankel, Michael, James Scouras, and George Ullrich, *Nonstrategic Nuclear Weapons at an Inflection Point*, Laurel, Md.: Johns Hopkins University Applied Physics Laboratory, 2017.

GAO—*See* U.S. General Accounting Office.

Garthoff, Raymond L. "New Soviet Thinking on Conflict Initiation, Control, and Termination," in Stephen J. Cimbala and Sidney R. Waldman, eds., *Controlling and Ending Conflict*, New York: Greenwood Press, 1992, pp. 65–94.

Gavin, Francis J., *Nuclear Statecraft: History and Strategy in America's Atomic Age*, Ithaca, N.Y.: Cornell University Press, 2012.

George, Alexander L., and Richard Smoke, *Deterrence in American Foreign Policy: Theory and Practice*, New York: Columbia University Press, 1974.

Getler, Michael, "Pershing II Missile: Why It Alarms Soviets," *Washington Post*, March 17, 1982. As of December 3, 3018:
https://www.washingtonpost.com/archive/politics/1982/03/17/pershing-ii-missile-why-it-alarms-soviets/20eca6f0-3a64-4bdf-9957-ae54261b6ca6/?noredirect=on&utm_term=.0d3144278ef0

Grau, Lester W., and Charles K. Bartles, *The Russian Way of War: Force Structure, Tactics, and Modernization of Russian Ground Forces*, Fort Leavenworth, Kan.: Foreign Military Studies Office, 2017.

Hagel, Chuck, "Statement on Strategic Choices and Management Review," Washington, D.C.: Office of the Secretary of Defense, July 31, 2013.

Heads of State and Government of the North Atlantic Alliance, "Warsaw Summit Communiqué," press release, Brussels: North Atlantic Treaty Organization, 2016.

Hines, John, Ellis M. Mishulovich, and John F. Shulle, *Soviet Intentions 1965–1985*, Vol. 1: *An Analytical Comparison of U.S.-Soviet Assessments During the Cold War*, McLean, Va.: BDM Federal, 1995. As of November 7, 2018:
https://nsarchive2.gwu.edu/nukevault/ebb285

Hyten, John E., "Statement Before the Senate Armed Services Committee," Washington, D.C.: U.S. Senate Armed Services Committee, March 20, 2018. As of November 12, 2018:
https://www.armed-services.senate.gov/imo/media/doc/Hyten_03-20-18.pdf

Ignatius, David, "Trump Hurls a Wrecking Ball at the Transatlantic Alliance," *Washington Post*, June 21, 2018.

Iklé, Fred C., "Can Nuclear Deterrence Last Out the Century?" *Foreign Affairs*, January 1973.

Jervis, Robert, Richard. N. Lebow, and Janet G. Stein, *Psychology and Deterrence*, Baltimore, Md.: Johns Hopkins University Press, 1985.

Johnson, Dave, *Nuclear Weapons in Russia's Approach to Conflict*, Paris: Foundation for Strategic Research, 2016.

———, *Russia's Conventional Precision Strike Capabilities, Regional Crises, and Nuclear Thresholds*, Livermore, Calif.: Lawrence Livermore National Laboratory, Center for Global Security Research, 2018.

Kahn, Herman, *On Thermonuclear War*, Princeton, N.J.: Princeton University Press, 1960.

———, *On Thermonuclear War: Metaphors and Scenarios*, New York: Praeger, 1965.

Kahneman, Daniel, "Maps of Bounded Rationality: A Perspective on Intuitive Judgment and Choice," Nobel Prize Lecture, Stockholm, 2002.

Kamp, Karl-Heinz, and Robertus C. N. Remkes, "Options for NATO Nuclear Sharing Arrangements," in Steve Andreasen and Isabelle Williams, eds., *Reducing Nuclear Risks in Europe: A Framework for Action*, Washingon, D.C.: Nuclear Threat Initiative, 2011, pp. 76–95.

Khrushchev, Sergei, ed., *Memoirs of Nikita Khrushchev*, Vol. 3: *Statesman, 1953–1964*, University Park, Pa.: Penn State University Press, 2007.

Kissinger, Henry, *Nuclear Weapons and Foreign Policy*, New York: Council on Foreign Relations, 1957.

———, "Domestic Structure and Foreign Policy," *Daedalus*, Vol. 95, No. 2, Spring 1966, pp. 503–529.

Kostrzewa–Zorbas, Grzegorz, "Россия хочет выигрывать войны с более слабыми противниками одной бомбой или боеголовкой [Russia Wants to Win a War with a Weaker Opponent with a Single Bomb or Warhead]," *wPolityce.pl*, June 2, 2016. As of November 29, 2018: https://inosmi.ru/military/20160602/236750638.html

Krepinevich, Andrew F., and Jacob Cohn, *Rethinking Armageddon: Scenario Planning in the Second Nuclear Age*, Washington, D.C.: Center for Strategic and Budgetary Assessments, 2016.

Krepinevich, Andrew F., and Barry D. Watts, *The Last Warrior: Andrew Marshall and the Shaping of Modern American Defense Strategy*, New York: Basic Books, 2015.

Kristensen, Hans M., *Non-Strategic Nuclear Weapons*, Federation of American Scientists, Special Report No. 3, May 2012. As of August 18, 2018: https://fas.org/_docs/Non_Strategic_Nuclear_Weapons.pdf

———, "B-52 Bomber No Longer Delivers Nuclear Gravity Bombs," Federation of American Scientists, May 25, 2017. As of August 18, 2018: https://fas.org/blogs/security/2017/05/b-52-bombs

Kristensen, Hans M., and Robert S. Norris, "The B61 Family of Nuclear Bombs," *Bulletin of the Atomic Scientists*, Vol. 70, No. 3, 2014, pp. 79–84.

Kroenig, Matthew, *Toward a More Flexible NATO Nuclear Posture: Developing a Response to a Russian Nuclear De-Escalation Strike*, Washington, D.C.: Atlantic Council, Issue Brief, November 2016.

Legge, J. Michael, *Theater Nuclear Weapons and the NATO Strategy of Flexible Response*, Santa Monica, Calif.: RAND Corporation, R-2964-FF, 2003. As of August 18, 2018:
https://www.rand.org/pubs/reports/R2964.html

Leites, Nathan, *Soviet Style in War*, Santa Monica, Calif.: RAND Corporation, R-2615-NA, 1992. As of November 7, 2018:
https://www.rand.org/pubs/reports/R2615-1.html

Levine, Robert, Thomas C. Schelling, and William Jones, *Crisis Games 27 Years Later: Plus C'est Déjà Vu*, Santa Monica, Calif.: RAND Corporation, P-7719, 1991. As of November 7, 2018:
https://www.rand.org/pubs/papers/P7719.html

Levshin, V. I., A. V. Nedelin, and M. E. Sosnovskii, "O primenenii yadernogo oruzhiya dlya deeskalatsii voennykh deistvii [On the Use of Nuclear Weapons for the De-Escalation of Hostilities]," *Voennaya Mysl'*, No. 3, May 1999.

Lostumbo, Michael J., Michael J. McNerney, Eric Peltz, Derek Eaton, David R. Frelinger, Victoria A. Greenfield, John Halliday, Patrick Mills, Bruce R. Nardulli, Stacie L. Pettyjohn, Jerry M. Sollinger, and Stephen M. Worman, *Overseas Basing of U.S. Military Forces: An Assessment of Relative Costs and Strategic Benefits*, Santa Monica, Calif.: RAND Corporation, RR-201-OSD, 2013. As of November 7, 2018:
https://www.rand.org/pubs/research_reports/RR201.html

Luik, Jüri, and Tomas Jermalavičius, "A Plausible Scenario of Nuclear War in Europe, and How to Deter It: A Perspective from Estonia," *Bulletin of the Atomic Scientists*, Vol. 73, No. 4, 2017, pp. 233–239.

Mahnken, Thomas G., ed., *Competitive Strategies for the 21st Century: Theory, History, and Practice*, Redwood City, Calif.: Stanford University Press, 2012.

Maisel, Adam, and Laurynas Keurakis, "Baltic Trainspotting: Railways and NATO's Logistics Problem in Northeasetern Europe," Modern War Institute at West Point, April 2, 2018.

Majumdar, Dave, "Everything You Need to Know: Russia's 'Tactical' Nuclear Weapons," *National Interest*, October 2017.

Marshall, A. W., *Long-Term Competition with the Soviets: A Framework for Strategic Analysis*, Santa Monica, Calif.: RAND Corporation, R-862-PR, 1972. As of August 18, 2018:
https://www.rand.org/pubs/reports/R862.html

McNamara, Eoin Micheál, "Securing the Nordic-Baltic Region," *NATO Review*, 2016. As of November 29, 2018:
https://www.nato.int/docu/review/2016/also-in-2016/security-baltic-defense-nato/EN/index.htm

Messmer, Marion, and Brad Roberts, *Adapting Deterrence Strategies to a Changing Security Environment*, Wilton Park, UK, August 2018. As of November 29, 2018:
https://www.wiltonpark.org.uk/wp-content/uploads/WP1610-Report.pdf

Miller, Franklin C., "The Nuclear Posture Review: Fiction and Fact," *Real Clear Defense*, February 20, 2018. As of November 7, 2018:
https://www.realcleardefense.com/articles/2018/02/20/the_nuclear_posture_review__fiction_and_fact_113080.html

Ministry of Defence of the Russian Federation, "Mission and Objectives of the Russian Armed Forces," webpage, undated. As of September 16, 2018:
http://eng.mil.ru/en/mission/tasks.htm

Morgan, Patrick M., *Deterrence Now*, Cambridge, UK: Cambridge University Press, 2003.

Narang, Vipin, *Nuclear Strategy in the Modern Era: Regional Powers and International Conflict*, Princeton, N.J.: Princeton University Press, 2014.

National Geospatial-Intelligence Agency, Automated Air Facilities Intelligence File, St. Louis, Mo., 2010, not available to the general public.

National Nuclear Security Administration, "B61-12 Life Extension Program," Fact Sheet, Washington, D.C.: U.S. Department of Energy, undated. As of November 12, 2018:
https://www.energy.gov/sites/prod/files/2018/02/f48/B61-12%20LEP%20factsheet.pdf

National Research Council, *U.S. Conventional Prompt Global Strike: Issues for 2008 and Beyond*, Washington, D.C.: National Academies Press, 2008.

———, *U.S. Air Force Strategic Deterrence Analytic Capabilities: An Assessment of Methods, Tools, and Approaches for the 21st Century Security Environment*, Washington, D.C.: National Academies Press, 2014.

NATO—See North Atlantic Treaty Organization.

Nichols, Tom, Douglas Stuart, and Jeffrey D. McCausland, eds., *Tactical Nuclear Weapons and NATO*, Carlisle Barracks, Pa.: Strategic Studies Institute, U.S. Army War College, 2012.

Norris, Robert S., and Hans M. Kristensen, "U.S. Tactical Nuclear Weapons in Europe," *Bulletin of the Atomic Scientists*, Vol. 67, No. 1, 2011, pp. 64–73.

North Atlantic Treaty Organization, *Active Engagement, Modern Defence: Strategic Concept for the Defence and Security of the Members of the North Atlantic Treaty Organization*, Brussels, 2010.

———, *Deterrence and Defence Posture Review*, Brussels, May 2012.

———, *NATO's Readiness Action Plan*, Fact Sheet, Brussels, 2016.

———, "NATO's Nuclear Deterrence Policy and Forces," webpage, May 17, 2018a. As of November 12, 2018:
https://www.nato.int/cps/en/natohq/topics_50068.htm?selectedLocale=en

———, "Brussels Summit Declaration," press release, PR/CP(2018)074, July 11, 2018b. As of November 12, 2018:
https://www.nato.int/nato_static_fl2014/assets/pdf/pdf_2018_07/20180713_180711-summit-declaration-eng.pdf

Office of Cost Assessment and Program Evaluation, *Operation and Support Cost-Estimating Guide*, Washington, D.C.: Office of the Secretary of Defense, March 2014.

Office of the Under Secretary of Defense (Comptroller), *European Reassurance Initiative: Department of Defense Budget Fiscal Year (FY) 2018*, Washington, D.C., May 2017.

———, *European Deterrence Initiative: Department of Defense Budget Fiscal Year (FY) 2019)*, Washington, D.C., February 2018.

Oliker, Olga, *Russia's Nuclear Doctrine: What We Know, What We Don't, and What That Means*, Washington, D.C.: Center for Strategic and International Studies, 2016.

Oliker, Olga, and Andrey Baklitskiy, "The Nuclear Posture Review and Russia 'De-Escalation': A Dangerous Solution to a Non-Existent Problem," *War on the Rocks*, February 20, 2018. As of June 14, 2018:
https://warontherocks.com/2018/02/nuclear-posture-review-russian-de-escalation-dangerous-solution-nonexistent-problem

Payne, Keith B., "Understanding Deterrence," *Comparative Strategy*, Vol. 30, No. 5, 2011, pp. 393–427.

Payne, Keith B., and John S. Foster, "Russian Strategy: Expansion, Crisis and Conflict," *Comparative Strategy*, Vol. 36, No. 1, May 2017.

Pechatnov, Y. A., "Analiz otechestvennykh i zarubezhnykh podkhodov k formirovaniyu kontseptsii i mekhanizma sderzhivaniya ot razvyazyvaniya voennoi agressii [Analysis of the Domestic and Foreign Approaches to the Formation of the Concept and Mechanism of Deterrence against the Outbreak of Military Aggression]," *Vooruzheniei Ekonomika*, Vol. 3, No. 11, 2010, pp. 11–17.

President of the Russian Federation, *The Military Doctrine of the Russian Federation*, Moscow, 2014. As of July 4, 2018:
https://rusemb.org.uk/press/2029

———, "Osnovy gosudarstvennoi politiki v oblasti voenno-morskoi deiatel'nosti do 2030 goda [Basic Principles of State Naval Policy in the Period to 2030]," July 20, 2017. As of September 14 2018:
http://kremlin.ru/acts/bank/42117

President's Foreign Intelligence Advisory Board, *The Soviet "War Scare,"* Washington, D.C.: George Washington University National Security Archive, February 15, 1990.

Putin, Vladimir, "Poslanie Vladimira Putina Federal'nomu sobraniiu 2018, Polnaia versiia, [2018 Address of Vladimir Putin to the Federal Assembly, Full Version]," *Pervyi Kanal*, March 1, 2018. As of June 14, 2018:
https://www.1tv.ru/shows/vystupleniya-prezidenta-rossii/poslanie-federalnomu-sobraniyu/poslanie-vladimira-putina-federalnomu-sobraniyu-2018-polnaya-versiya

RAND Corporation, "Robust Decision Making," webpage, undated. As of November 12, 2018:
https://www.rand.org/topics/robust-decision-making.html

———, *Fostering Innovation in the Defense Department: Examples from RAND's Federally Funded Research and Development Centers*, Santa Monica, Calif., CP-852, 2016. As of November 12, 2018:
https://www.rand.org/pubs/corporate_pubs/CP852.html

Reagan, Ronald, *An American Life*, New York: Simon & Schuster, 1990.

Roberts, Brad, *The Case for U.S. Nuclear Weapons in the 21st Century*, Redwood City, Calif.: Stanford University Press, 2015.

Savranskaya, Svetlana, and David A. Welch, eds., *SALT II and the Growth of Mistrust: Transcript of the Proceedings of the Musgrave Conference of the Carter-Brezhnev Project*, St. Simon's Island, Ga.: Musgrave Plantation, February 5, 1995.

Schelling, Thomas C., *The Strategy of Conflict*, Cambridge, Mass.: Harvard University Press, 1960.

———, "The Role of War Games and Exercises," in Ashton B. Carter, John D. Steinbruner, and Charles A. Zraket, eds., *Managing Nuclear Operations*, Washington, D.C.: Brookings Institution Press, 1987, pp. 426–444.

Schlesinger, James, *The Theater Nuclear Force Posture in Europe: A Report to the United States Congress in Compliance with Public Law 93-365*, Washington, D.C.: U.S. Department of Defense, 1975.

Schneider, Mark B., "Escalate to De-Escalate," *Proceedings Magazine*, Vol. 143, No. 2, 2017, p. 1368.

Schulte, Paul, "Tactical Nuclear Weapons in NATO and Beyond: A Historical and Thematic Examination," in Tom Nichols, Douglas Stuart, and Jeffrey D. McCausland, eds., *Tactical Nuclear Weapons and NATO*, Carlisle Barracks, Pa.: Strategic Studies Institute, U.S. Army War College, 2012, pp. 13–74.

Schwartz, Stephen I., *Atomic Audit: The Costs and Consequences of U.S. Nuclear Weapons Since 1940*, Washington, D.C.: Brookings Institution Press, June 1, 1998.

Sengupta, Kim, "Russia's Grip on Europe's Oil Supply Threatens Ukraine's Energy Independence," *Independent*, May 2, 2017. As of November 7, 2018: https://www.independent.co.uk/news/world/europe/russia-ukraine-gas-energy-supply-solution-putin-holds-key-a7714141.html

Shlapak, David A., and Michael W. Johnson, *Reinforcing Deterrence on NATO's Eastern Flank: Wargaming the Defense of the Baltics*, Santa Monica, Calif.: RAND Corporation, RR-1253-A, 2016. As of August 18, 2018: https://www.rand.org/pubs/research_reports/RR1253.html

Slocombe, Walter B., "The Countervailing Strategy," *International Security*, Vol. 5, No. 4, 1981, pp. 18–27.

Sokolovsky, V. D., *Soviet Military Strategy*, New York: Taylor & Francis Group, 1984.

Sokov, Nikolai, *Russia's Nuclear Doctrine*, Washington, D.C.: Nuclear Threat Initiative, 2004.

———, "Russian Perspective on Non-Strategic Nuclear Weapons," in Tom Nichols, Douglas Stuart, and Jeffrey D. McCausland, eds., *Tactical Nuclear Weapons and NATO*, Carlisle Barracks, Pa.: Strategic Studies Institute, U.S. Army War College, 2012, pp. 199–226.

———, "Why Russia Calls a Limited Nuclear Strike 'De-Escalation,'" *Bulletin of the Atomic Scientists*, March 13, 2014.

Taylor, Adam, and Michael Birnbaum, "NATO Allies Respond to Trump's Suggestion That the U.S. Might Not Protect Them from Russia," *Washington Post*, July 21, 2016.

Tellis, Ashley J., C. Christine Fair, and Jamison Jo Medby, *Limited Conflicts Under the Nuclear Umbrella: Indian and Pakistani Lessons from the Kargil Crisis*, Santa Monica, Calif.: RAND Corporation, MR-1450-USCA, 2001. As of November 7, 2018: https://www.rand.org/pubs/monograph_reports/MR1450.html

Tetrais, Bruno, "Russia's Nuclear Policy: Worrying for the Wrong Reason," *Survival*, Vol. 60, No. 2, 2018, pp. 33–44.

"Text of Accounts by Lucas and Considine in Interviews with MacArthur in 1954," *New York Times*, April 9, 1964. As of November 7, 2018: http://www.nytimes.com/1964/04/09/texts-of-accounts-by-lucas-and-considine-on-interviews-with-macarthur-in-1954.html

United States and Russia, Treaty Between the United States of America and the Russian Federation on Measures for the Further Reduction and Limitations of Strategic Offensive Arms, Prague, April 8, 2010.

United States and Soviet Union, Treaty Between the United States of America and the Union of Soviet Socialist Republics on the Elimination of Their Intermediate-Range and Shorter-Range Missiles, Washington, D.C., December 8, 1987.

U.S. Department of Defense, *Selected Acquisition Report: ATACMS-BAT,* Washington, D.C., December 2002.

———, *Selected Acquisition Report (SAR): B61 Mod 12 Life Extension Program (B61-12 LEP)*, Washington, D.C., June 2013a.

———, *Selected Acquisition Report (SAR): W76 Mod 1 Life Extension Program (W76-1 LEP)*, Washington, D.C., June 2013b.

———, *Selected Acquisition Report (SAR): B61 Mod 12 Life Extension Program Tailkit Assembly (B61-12 LEP TKA)*, Washington, D.C., December 2016.

———, *Selected Acquisition Report: Tactical Tomahawk RGM-109E/UGM-109E Missile (TACTOM)*, Washington, D.C., December 2017.

———, *Nuclear Posture Review*, Washington, D.C., 2018.

U.S. Department of Defense Inspector General, *Evaluation of the European Reassurance Initiative (ERI)*, Washington, D.C., DODIG 2017-111, August 22, 2017.

U.S. Department of Energy, *Department of Energy FY2018 Congressional Budget Request, National Nuclear Security Administration, Federal Salaries and Expenses, Weapon Activities, Defense Nuclear Nonproliferation, Naval Reactors*, Washington, D.C., May 2017.

U.S. Department of State, *U.S. Nuclear Employment Strategy*, Fact Sheet, October 6, 2016.

U.S. General Accounting Office, *INF Treaty: Cost of Weapon Systems to Be Destroyed and Possible Savings*, Washington, D.C., NSIAD-88-141FS, March 24, 1988.

———, *INF Treaty: Army and Air Force Personnel Reductions*, Washington, D.C., NSIAD-89-173FS, 1989.

U.S. Strategic Command, *Deterrence Operations Joint Operating Concept*, Washington, D.C.: U.S. Department of Defense, December 2006.

Velez-Green, Alexander, *The Unsettling View from Moscow: Russia's Strategic Debate on a Doctrine of Pre-Emption*, Washington, D.C.: Center for a New American Security, April 2018. As of November 7, 2018: https://s3.amazonaws.com/files.cnas.org/documents/CNASReport-RussiaStrike-Finalb.pdf?mtime=20170428143631

Wohlstetter, Albert, "The Delicate Balance of Terror," *Foreign Affairs*, Vol. 37, No. 2, 1959, pp. 211–234.

———, "The Political and Military Aims of Offense and Defense Innovation," in Fred S. Hoffman, Albert Wohlstetter, and David S. Yost, eds., *Swords and Shields: NATO, the USSR, and New Choices for Long-Range Offense and Defense*, Lexington, Mass.: Lexington Books, 1987.

Woods, Kevin M., *The Mother of All Battles: Saddam Hussein's Strategic Plan for the Persian Gulf War*, Newport, R.I.: Naval Institute Press, 2008.

Woods, Kevin M., Williamson Murray, Elizabeth A. Nathan, Laila Sabara, and Ana M. Venegas, *Saddam's Generals: Perspectives of the Iran-Iraq War*, Alexandria, Va.: Institute for Defense Analyses, 2011.

Woodward, Robert, *The Commanders*, New York: Simon & Schuster, 1991.

Work, Robert O., and James A. Winnefeld, "Testimony Before the Committee on Armed Services, U.S. House of Representatives," Washington, D.C., June 25, 2015.

Zysk, Katarzyna, "Nonstrategic Nuclear Weapons in Russia's Evolving Nuclear Doctrine," *Bulletin of the Atomic Scientists*, Vol. 73, No. 5, 2017, pp. 322–327.

———, "Escalation and Nuclear Weapons in Russia's Military Strategy," *RUSI Journal*, Vol. 163, No. 2, 2018.

# Author Bios

**Paul K. Davis** is a principal researcher at the RAND Corporation and a professor of policy analysis at the Pardee RAND Graduate School. His research interests include strategic planning, national security strategy, decisionmaking, deterrence, and integrative methods of qualitative and quantitative analysis and modeling.

**J. Michael Gilmore** is a researcher at the Institute for Defense Analyses. Previously, he was a principal researcher at the RAND Corporation and held several positions in the U.S. government, including director of Operational Test and Evaluation at DoD. His research interests focus on quantitative analyses informing decisionmaking on national security issues.

**David R. Frelinger** is a senior policy researcher at the RAND Corporation. His work has focused on developing appropriate responses to homeland security threats generated from the use of advanced and novel weapons, stability and counterinsurgency, simulation and modeling, information technologies, and advanced weapon system concepts and operations.

**Edward Geist** is an associate policy researcher at the RAND Corporation. His research interests include the former Soviet Union, nuclear weapons, emergency management, cybersecurity, and modeling of nuclear weapon effects.

**Chris Gilmore** is a forward-deployed engineer with C3.ai and a former associate engineer at the RAND Corporation, where his research interests included defense technology and energy and environmental policy.

**Jenny Oberholtzer** is a defense analyst at the RAND Corporation. She focuses on emerging and novel threats to the United States' and allies' interests, the building of robust systems, and the design of wargames.

**Danielle C. Tarraf** is a senior information scientist at the RAND Corporation. Her project work at RAND has two primary themes: information-based defense technologies and modeling and analysis of strategic interactions to inform decisionmaking under uncertainty.